When a Parent Is Very Sick

When a Parent Is Very Sick

by Eda LeShan

Illustrated by
Jacqueline Rogers

The Atlantic Monthly Press
BOSTON   NEW YORK

FIRST EDITION

Library of Congress Cataloging-in-Publication Data

LeShan, Eda J.
  When a parent is very sick.

  Summary: Discusses typical feelings and incidents
encountered by a child when a parent is seriously ill or
hurt, as well as how it affects the entire family, and
suggests ways to deal with such situations.
  1. Parent and child—Juvenile literature. 2. Sick—
Family relationships—Juvenile literature. 3. Parents—
Death—Psychological aspects—Juvenile literature.
[1. Sick—Family relationships. 2. Parent and child.
3. Family problems] I. Title.
BF723.P25L45 1986   155.9′3   86-3523
ISBN 0-87113-095-5

BP

Published simultaneously in Canada

PRINTED IN THE UNITED STATES OF AMERICA

For Larry,
in recognition of the thousands
of sick parents as well as their children
to whom he has dedicated
so much of his life

With special gratitude to Marvin Meitus, M.D.,
Wendy LeShan, Jo-ann Straat, and Lawrence LeShan

Contents

Introduction

Adam's father has come home early. It's only four o'clock in the afternoon and Adam has been waiting nervously since getting home from school to find out how his mother is. She has been in the hospital for two days having some tests because she hasn't been feeling well for several weeks. Adam has been having a very hard time concentrating on his third-grade homework. When he sees his father coming from the driveway to the front door, he gets up to meet him, but his father rushes past Adam and goes to the phone. His father looks terrible. He says, "Hi, Adam, have you done your homework? I'll talk to you later." He calls Adam's grandmother. Adam hears him say, in a shaking voice, "Elizabeth? It's not good. They'll have to operate as soon as possible.

Yes, I think you'd better come." Then his father calls his boss. He speaks to the secretary. "Just tell Paul I will be out for the next few days. I'll let him know what happens." Adam feels his heart beating fast. He is so frightened. He begins to feel very angry at his father, who wants to talk to other people when he should be talking to Adam.

Alison comes home from school and is startled to see her parents sitting on the living room couch, holding hands and crying. They hold their arms out to her. Her mother says, "It's all right, darling. Don't get frightened. We're just worried because the doctor wants Daddy to have some special treatments that will make Daddy feel quite sick for a while." Alison knows her father has cancer but she thought he was getting better. This must mean he's getting worse. She pushes her mother away and runs into her brother's room, crying. Walter is lying on his bed staring at the ceiling, and turns his face to the wall when he sees Alison.

When Barbara and David get off the school bus they notice that Aunt Bea's car is in front of their apartment house. When they open the door, Aunt Bea rushes toward them and throws her arms around them. "Oh, my poor babies!" she says. "You must be very brave and not upset your mother when she comes home." Barbara, who is only five years old, starts to cry. David, who is nine, shouts at his aunt: "What are you *talking* about?" His mother was just fine when she kissed him good-bye and gave him his lunch box after breakfast. Aunt Bea says, "David, I don't like you to shout at me. Your mother was in a car accident and she was taken to a hospital. You mustn't upset her when Daddy brings her home tomorrow."

In all these cases the children know that something terrible is happening. Now the same kind of thing has happened to you. Like these other children, you are probably very frightened. You understand just how these children are feeling. It makes sense to you to be frightened if a parent is ill or hurt. What probably makes you very uncomfortable is some of the other kinds of feelings you may be having. Feeling angry is just as natural as feeling frightened.

Most of all, a child is likely to feel helpless. There is nothing you can do to make this awful thing go away. That may be true, but you are not as helpless as you think. There are ways in which you can become strong enough to help yourself and your family, and that is what this book is all about.

When a Parent
Is Very Sick

1

When You Find Out Something Terrible Has Happened

When a child is very, very young he or she feels completely dependent on parents for everything. Children need to believe — and do believe — that parents are strong and brave and wise and will always take care of them. You *have* to believe that when you are an infant or a toddler, because you really are helpless and couldn't possibly take care of yourself even for a day. Little children think parents have almost magical powers to keep them safe from harm.

Now you are probably old enough to know that parents aren't perfect. You have discovered they don't always understand how you are feeling; sometimes they can be impatient and angry and unfair. Sometimes they seem sad and sometimes they seem to you to do very foolish things. Charlie just can't understand why his father makes such a fuss because he forgot to close the garage door; Connie wishes her mother wouldn't go to a PTA meeting wearing such ugly green slacks; and Alex is very surprised to discover that his teacher knows much more about astronomy than his father. As we get older we all discover that our parents are human beings and that there is no such thing as a perfect person.

But in spite of discovering that parents are not always strong and wise and brave, it is still a shock to discover that a parent can become so sick that there are times when he or she can't take care of you. Your parents have probably had the flu or maybe a sprained ankle or an upset stomach, but this time it is different. And the reason it is so upsetting is that somewhere, deep inside of you, there is still a little kid who thought parents would always be able to take care of you.

Changes That Are Frightening

Suddenly something awful is happening. Everything has changed. It feels as if nothing will ever be the same. Life has suddenly become frightening and dangerous.

Not only may your parents seem different, but so may all the other people around you. When her mother got sick, Amanda couldn't understand why

her father stopped talking to her and spent the evenings alone in his bedroom. Josh had never seen his
grandfather cry before and it scared him. Some people who came to his house cried and wanted to hug
him. Other people ignored him and seemed very
quiet and far away, even in the same room. When
he went into the dining room, where his mother
was sitting, she acted as if nothing was wrong. She
smiled and asked him about school, and never said
a word about having to go to the hospital for an
operation.

Some people seem to know just what to say and
understand how you are feeling. Other people seem
to make you feel worse. People who tell you you
must be brave and strong make you feel scared and
weak. When Grandma walks around the apartment
wringing her hands and crying and goes around saying, "Oh, my poor babies!" every time she looks at
you or your brother, you feel angry at her. On the
other hand, the next-door neighbor may turn out to
be the biggest help of all. Perhaps she meets you
on your way to school when you are feeling terrible,
and she puts a hand on your shoulder and says,
"What is happening is awful and I know how scared
you are, but I want you to know you will never,
ever, be alone — many, many people love you and
will take care of you."

It is hard enough to deal with your own feelings,
much less try to understand other people's, but it

will help if you do try to figure out why people are doing the things they are doing. People behave differently in different situations because they have different personalities. They grew up in different homes with different kinds of parents. Amanda's father was taught when he was a little boy that boys and men don't cry; he goes into the bedroom so that Amanda won't see him cry, because he's ashamed. Josh's grandfather grew up in a family where people felt free to express their feelings and so he expresses his feelings very easily. When he's very happy he grabs Grandma and dances around the living room; when he's sad he cries. Josh's mother covered up her feelings, thinking she could protect Josh from being frightened and worried. She was wrong, but nobody had ever tried to help her understand that it is never a good idea to shut a child out when something bad is happening.

It can also help to remember how people behaved *before* your mother or father got sick. Maybe Grandma always carries on a lot when she is upset. You may remember that she screamed and cried for two whole days when her brother died — but after that she was wonderful, comforting her sister-in-law, arranging for the funeral, taking care of her two nieces. She may just be the kind of person who goes to pieces at first, but is then able to pull herself together and help everyone else.

Martin's father comes home, sits down to watch

a football game on television, and drinks several cans of beer, while Mom is in the hospital. At first Martin gets very angry at his father. Then, when he thinks about it, he realizes that that's what his father *always* does when he's upset. Phyllis is furious when Aunt Ellen says, "How about a game of Monopoly?" At first she thinks Aunt Ellen just doesn't care, or doesn't understand how sick Daddy is. When Phyllis angrily says, "How can you think about playing a game?" Aunt Ellen looks as if somebody had punched her in the stomach. "I'm sorry, darling," she says, "I didn't mean to be thoughtless. I just thought it might be a relief to take your mind off your worries for a little while."

What may be hardest of all is when your parents themselves seem to change in the way they react to each other. Maria sees that her mother and father argue much more than they used to, even though her mother doesn't feel well. One day she hears them screaming at each other about whether or not they should get another medical opinion. It may help Maria if she can try to understand that when grown-ups are frightened they sometimes act more angry. The truth is they are just very worried.

Sometimes a parent's sickness may mean he or she gets very depressed. This is called a mental illness, coming mostly from mixed-up thoughts and feelings. Edward's mother doesn't want to talk to him at all. She doesn't even seem to care when he tells her that he got an A in arithmetic. She just keeps looking out the window. He can hear her crying in bed at night. His father tries to make her eat some supper, but she just closes her mouth. Edward feels anxious and thinks his mother just doesn't love him anymore. The truth is that his mother is suffering from a mental illness, which means that she is sick in her feelings. Right now she is too upset to be able to think about Edward and he feels very hurt and alone.

New Kinds of Feelings

Whatever the illness a parent may have, it brings on many different kinds of feelings for a child. Sometimes children think their feelings are very strange and unnatural, but there are really no feelings that are not normal when something terrible has happened.

The first feeling most children have (and grownups, too) is a feeling of shock; you just can't believe what is happening. This is particularly true if the something bad happens very suddenly. Carrie told her teacher, "One minute my mother was standing next to me at the bus stop and the next minute she was lying on the ground, hit by a car with a drunken driver. All my mind kept thinking was, No, this didn't happen." The shock can be so great you just feel as if your mind has stopped working altogether.

This can happen even if you have known for some time that a parent has been sick. Juan was eight years old when he found out that his mother had a heart condition. She had to rest a great deal. After a while Juan got used to his mother's illness, but even so, when she had a bad heart attack when Juan was twelve, it was still a shock.

The second natural reaction to a parent's illness is fear. Susan felt very ashamed that the thing she kept thinking about the most was not how much pain her mother was having after an operation, but who would take care of *her*. That is a normal feeling. It didn't mean that Susan didn't care about her mother. Being scared makes all children worry about who will take care of them, because they know they are not old enough to take care of themselves. Karen was ashamed that instead of thinking about her father's illness, she kept thinking, "If he can't work anymore, what will happen to me?" That is a real question and nothing to feel ashamed about.

When someone you love gets sick it reminds you of times when you've been sick. You remember feeling so awful when you had the flu that nothing else mattered but the pain in your head or throwing up. Vanessa told her aunt Elyse, "When I was sick I didn't care what happened to anyone else. Is that the way Daddy feels?" Aunt Elyse reminded Vanessa, "But as soon as you felt better, you stopped feeling that way, didn't you? It's true that right now

Daddy is thinking mostly about whether or not he will have to have chemotherapy for the tumor in his neck, but you can be sure that as soon as he knows what has to be done, he will think about his family again."

It's also normal to wonder if you might get the same disease your parent has. Louise wondered if you could catch hepatitis; Bill worried that cancer might be hereditary, and that he might get it when he was his mother's age. And perhaps the biggest fear of all is that a parent might die. All these fears are natural.

It is also normal to feel guilty. Emily is sure that the reason her mother is so sick is that Emily hasn't been nice to her; recently they seemed to be fighting about a lot of things and Emily had shouted, "I hate you!" at her mother when she'd refused to let her go to a party where there weren't going to be any grown-ups. Emily needs to remember that she is twelve years old, and at that age almost all girls fight with their mothers! It's a time when young people need to begin to become more independent and it is also a time when they want desperately to be exactly like their friends. The arguments had nothing whatever to do with Emily's mother's illness. If Emily were to ask her mother about it, her mother would probably laugh and hug her and say, "You're becoming an adolescent and that's probably going to be hard on both of us sometimes, but I know you

love me, and I love you, and the reason I'm sick is
my own fault — I should have stopped smoking a
long time ago."

One time when Oscar was sitting at the dining
room table at suppertime, and kicking the leg of the
table, his father got very angry and shouted, "You're
driving me crazy!" Later when Oscar is told that his
father has to go to the hospital because he's had a
mental breakdown, Oscar is positive it happened
because he was too noisy and too restless. What he
needs to understand is that his father had another
period of mental illness when he was in college,
many years before, and that what is happening now
is happening because his father was working much
too hard, became very irritable at his office, and was
fired. Probably the reason he got so angry at Oscar
for kicking the table was that he was overtired and
worried about not having a job.

When Richard found out that his mother might
die from leukemia, he was sure he knew exactly
why. One day when he and his younger sister were
having one of their usual fights, and he'd been teas-
ing her and pretending to take away her doll, his
mother had screamed at him, "You'll be the death
of me!" And she had been right, Richard thinks; his
being mean to his sister had done this awful thing
to her. *Wrong!* All brothers and sisters fight sometimes, and all parents get exasperated. If every time
a parent said "You'll be the death of me" it really

happened, there wouldn't be very many parents left! Both parents and children say things when they are angry that they don't really mean at all. A child never has the power to make a parent get sick. There are always many, many reasons for a serious illness, none of them the fault of a child.

Another normal reaction when a parent is very sick is to feel very angry. Debbie was furious at her mother for being hurt in a car accident; her mother had not been wearing her safety belt, and Debbie wanted to scream at her, "How could you do such a stupid and terrible thing to me?" When Larry found out his father would have to rest quietly for several months, he felt very angry. His father had been teaching him how to be a better catcher on his Little League team; now he wouldn't be any help at all. Larry was ashamed of being so angry. But feeling angry and resentful is normal when we are frightened or disappointed. It is better to let yourself know the way you're feeling than to try to cover up your feelings. Admitting you feel angry will make it easier to deal with your disappointments and frustrations.

The kind of anger that can be most upsetting when your parent is sick is the feeling, "I wish this had happened to Daddy instead of Mom. I feel so angry that she did this to me." Gregory felt this way. His father has a terrible temper and sometimes hits his sister and him, hard. His mother is the one who stops his father and now that she's sick his father is even more violent.

Rachel gets along fine with her father, who calls her his "little princess." Her troubles are with her mother, who's always nagging her about cleaning up her room. Now she feels angry that it is her father who is sick instead of her mother. Believe it or not, these are normal feelings, too! The way we know they are normal is that almost every child who has to face a parent's illness or death has such feelings. Sometimes, as in Gregory's case, there are very good reasons for such resentment, and he needs to tell someone about what is a serious problem. Other times we just have to realize that we love our parents differently at different times, and it is natural to think that some other arrangement might have been easier than the way things are.

Another kind of feeling that occurs is a feeling of helplessness. There doesn't seem to be anything you can do about what is happening. But that is not really true. Adam, who felt so left out when his father came home and started making telephone calls to tell other people what was happening to his mother and ignored Adam, waited until his father finished his phone calls and went into the kitchen to make a cup of coffee. Adam began to cry and ran after his father. He said, "You have to tell me what's happening!" His father looked startled. "I really *did* forget about you. I'm sorry," he said. He then sat down at the kitchen table and told Adam that his mother had a lump in her breast and that they had just found out it was malignant, which meant it was cancer. Now they had to talk to several different doctors to decide what would be the best treatment. Adam asked, "Will she die?" His father put his arm around Adam's shoulders and said, "The doctors say there is an excellent chance she can be completely cured." Sometimes taking action may mean letting a parent know how you feel. Crying can be a way of taking action. You are letting grown-ups know how worried you are and that you need comforting and information. Taking action may be letting a parent know that you will be able to deal with this problem much better if you know what's going on.

Ways of Helping Others and Yourself

Alison, who found her parents crying and who ran into her brother's room, wasn't helpless either. The next day she and her brother, Walter, went to see their father's doctor after school. He told them the truth: their father was having a recurrence of cancer. The treatments would make him feel pretty sick for a while. His hair would probably fall out and he might feel sick to his stomach. Alison and Walter were very quiet walking home. They passed a sporting-goods store and Walter said they should buy their father a baseball hat to wear if his hair really did fall out. His father loved the hat. The children told their parents they now knew what was happening. Alison said, "If Daddy has to throw up, I wouldn't mind helping. Remember when Buttons was a puppy and I had to clean him up when he was sick? I can do that."

At first their mother started to say, "That's very sweet of you, but you don't have to . . ." and then she looked very thoughtful for a moment. She said, "You're wonderful kids and you can help a lot. You can help me change Daddy's bed every day, and it would be terrific if you could read to Daddy when he's resting." Alison and Walter didn't feel helpless anymore.

David, the nine-year-old who got so angry at his aunt Bea, felt helpless about what she had done. She had made David feel that all she was thinking about was his mother, and not about his feelings. The next day when Daddy brought Mom home with a cast on one leg and another on her arm, David ran into his room and wouldn't come out to say hello to her. A little later his father came into the room. "Mom feels bad that you didn't say hello to her," he said. David explained. "Aunt Bea told me I had to be brave and not upset Mom," he said, "and I'm afraid I might start crying." His father hugged him and said, "Aunt Bea was wrong. Some things are worth crying about. Mom would be more upset if she thought you didn't want to see her." David, his little sister, Barbara, and their father went and sat on their mother's bed and they all had a good cry together. Then they began to make plans for what they could do to take care of things until Mom could walk again. David said, "I want to be in charge of making hamburgers!" Everyone agreed that would be great.

Bruce, who found out his mother had multiple sclerosis and would need to be in a wheelchair, learned over a long period of time what she could do and what she couldn't do. He found out that many relatives and friends wanted to help. Pretty soon he realized that life would go on; that while he had some new household chores — he and his father could cook supper and go shopping, and he could make his own sandwiches for lunch — Grandma could take him to the dentist, and sometimes he could visit his grandparents for a weekend, and Grandpa could take him to the high school football game, and he could be in charge of doing his homework without being nagged. He discovered he wasn't helpless. After the first shock of a parent's serious illness, life does go on.

2

Getting Ready to Deal with a Parent's Illness

As you begin to accept the fact that your mother or father is seriously ill, and after the first wave of strong and mixed-up feelings, what usually happens is that you want to know exactly what is going on. And the problem is that other people sometimes don't seem to be ready to tell you what you need to know, or they seem too preoccupied to sit down and talk.

Hilary said, "What grown-ups don't seem to understand is that a child can imagine much worse things than the truth!" Hilary's mother was in a car accident. It was raining very hard and a bus crashed into her when its brakes didn't work. Hilary heard her father talking to her grandmother on the phone and her father said, "The worst part is her back."

Right away Hilary thought something terrible had happened to her mother's spine. She knew that people could get paralyzed from such an injury, so she was scared to death. She tried to ask her father what he meant, but all he said was, "It's OK, kitten, everything will be all right. I have to get back to the hospital now that Mrs. Smith is here to take care of you. I'll talk to you tomorrow morning." All that night Hilary couldn't sleep. She kept thinking her mother would never be able to walk again. The next morning her father told her, "Mom has a big gash in her back from broken glass, but it's a flesh wound and although she'll have a scar, she'll be fine. It's just that she was having so much pain yesterday." Hilary felt so relieved, but she was also angry at her father for not explaining sooner.

When Jacob heard his father had had a heart attack, he was sure his father was going to die. Everyone was running around, and no one was paying any attention to him. He asked his mother and his grandfather when his father could come home; he asked his uncle what happened when a person had a heart attack. Everyone said, "Your father will be fine, there's nothing to worry about." But since everyone seemed upset and excited, he was sure they were just trying to protect him from the truth. The next day, in school, he started to cry on the playground; he just couldn't help himself. The teacher took him to the school nurse, who called Jacob's family doctor.

When she got through talking on the phone, she said, "Jacob, it's really true that your father will be all right. It was a slight heart attack that did not seriously damage his heart. He has been working too hard, and smoking, and he is overweight and doesn't get enough exercise. Now that he's had this warning, and knows he will have to take better care of himself, he will probably be healthier than before! You can help a lot by taking long walks with him and not asking him to take you to fast-food restaurants where he can't eat properly."

Like Hilary, Jacob was also relieved. As he walked back to his classroom he thought about telling his mom not to buy any more Twinkies and potato chips and soda, and wondered if it would be good for his father to play basketball with him in the yard where they had put up a hoop. He decided he'd ask the doctor later on when his father was better.

Protecting Children Doesn't Usually Help

Sometimes grown-ups try very hard to protect children because they think the truth will just be too painful. When Ronnie's father had a heart attack, his mother and his grandparents — even the doctor — told Larry his father wasn't very sick and would get all better. A few weeks later his father died. Then Ronnie found out that from the very beginning no one had expected his father to recover. The shock of his father's dying, when he didn't have any idea this might happen, was terrible. Ronnie cried and cried, and he screamed at his mother, "You didn't give me a chance to say good-bye! I could have told him how much I loved him." It is always a terrible thing for a child when a parent dies, but it was even more awful for Larry because he felt betrayed; in trying to protect him, people he loved had lied to him.

It is natural for parents to want to protect their children from pain and suffering. But sometimes they don't realize that when a parent is seriously ill there is really no way to keep a child from hurting, and that being included in what is happening is more comforting than being left out.

Getting Information

One of the first things you can do when you find out your parent is sick is to try to find people who will talk to you, people who are willing to give you simple and honest answers to your questions. Sometimes this will be a parent or another relative. Sometimes it could be your pediatrician or family doctor. Or it might be the school nurse or the school social worker or psychologist, if there are such people in your school. Or you might get in touch with organizations like Cancer Care that help families at times of crisis.* You need to think hard about who the people are that you trust the most and who have been honest and caring in the past.

Robert went to talk to his second-grade teacher, even though he was in fifth grade. He said, "I really loved Mrs. Munson, and she would smile and even hug me, sometimes, in the hall at school. I just felt comfortable talking to her." Diane said, "It was really strange. Sometimes it's surprising who turns out to help. I had to go to the drugstore to get a prescription filled for my father, and I started to cry. I've known the pharmacist since I was really little, and he was always very friendly and kind. When I started to cry, he came around the counter and put his arms around me, and then he told me what 'lupus' meant, and the different kinds there are, and the different symptoms, and how certain treatments could help a lot and many people had remissions for long periods of time. He explained that a chronic disease is one that never goes away completely and that remissions are periods when a person feels really well in spite of the disease not going away altogether. It wasn't that he made me think everything was all right, but I felt better because now I understood what was happening."

Sometimes we need to try to convince grown-ups that the truth is easier to deal with than not knowing. But the trouble with "the truth" is that often when

---

* These organizations are listed at the end of this book.

someone is very ill there is no such thing. Trudy
got very angry at the doctor who was taking care of
her mother, who had something called multiple
myeloma, a form of cancer. Trudy wanted to know
whether her mother was going to get well or whether
she might die; she wanted to know how long it would
take if her mother was going to get better. When
she met the doctor in the lobby of the hospital she
gathered up all her courage and said, "Dr. Schwartz,
I'm almost thirteen years old and people are treating
me like a baby. It's *my mother* and I have a right
to know what's going on!" Dr. Schwartz said, "I
know how you feel, Trudy, and I wish I could tell
you exactly what will happen, but I can't. Every
person is different, and even if two people have the
same disease, we can never be sure what is going
to happen. People react differently to medication.
What helps one person might not help someone
else. Somebody who we think will probably die may
recover completely. Somebody we are sure is going
to get well may get much worse. Every day we learn
more and discover better treatments, but human
beings are so complicated that there is no way we
can be sure what will happen."

Often "We just don't know" *is* the truth, and that
can be very upsetting. It can make you very angry
and anxious. It may make you feel angry at the
doctor. You think the doctor *should* be able to make
a parent well. All you can do in this case is to let

yourself feel your feelings. Things get much worse if you try *not* to feel angry and *not* to feel anxious. Trying not to feel a certain way can use up so much of your energy that it makes you tired all the time and unable to concentrate in school.

For some children learning as much as possible about a disease helps them feel better. George went to the school librarian and asked her for books about muscular dystrophy. She didn't have any, but she called the public library and asked if they might have any books for young people on this disease. The librarian at the public library said she only had adult textbooks but if George came over, she would read about it herself and try to explain what she read. She also suggested that there was a national organization on muscular dystrophy, and George could write to them for information. George was just the kind of person who feels better, the more facts he knows.

But it isn't always a relief to find out. Sometimes a child may think he wants to know the diagnosis and then feel sorry later on. Phillip said, "I kept asking everybody what was the matter with my dad, and nobody would give me a name for his illness. And then my aunt told me, and I was sorry I'd asked because then I was more scared than ever." Toni said, "I guess I have an ostrich personality. I just didn't want to hear the word for what was the matter with my mother. As long as I didn't hear the word

I felt as if she would get better." Each person is different. What we need to do all through our lives is to try to understand ourselves well enough so that we can tell what will make us feel better or worse. Some people need to know as much as possible; other people get more upset if they have too many facts.

The Relationship Between Feelings and Being Sick

There are some important things we know about every disease. We know, for example, that there is no separation at all between the body and the mind. Sickness and wellness happen to a whole person. This is the meaning of the word *psychosomatic*. Even with things that happen on the outside of a person, like breaking a leg or getting burned, the mind and the body are inseparable because the rate of healing will be influenced by feelings. As a matter of fact, even if a person gets a broken leg, the way in which it heals will have as much to do with the mind as with the body. Our brains send messages to every part of our bodies — through our glands and our hormones and all kinds of chemicals that work together. When you begin to study biology in school, you will be learning about all the fascinating signals and messages that go from one part of us to another part. For example, when something frightening or dangerous happens, a hormone named adrenaline is released into the body. It gives us more energy and makes it possible for us to handle a shock or pain more effectively. That's why people who are badly hurt often don't begin to feel pain until they get medical attention.

Worry and fear can change what goes on inside a person. When a person gets an ulcer in the stomach, this is due to the fact that the body is secreting more acid into the stomach than the stomach can deal with. It tells the person that he or she is under too much stress, has too many things to worry about, isn't paying attention to his or her health.

Your mind and body have been working together all your life! When you were a tiny baby you cried when you felt hungry; it *hurt!* As soon as you were fed, the pain went away and you didn't start crying again until you needed more food. The first day you went to school, you might have been so nervous that you threw up after breakfast. Your body was reacting to your feelings of nervousness. And the day you knew you had failed an arithmetic test and you had to tell your parents, you might have gotten a terrible headache.

Sergio said, "A funny thing happened to me. I didn't want to go to school because I had a teacher who yelled at us and made fun of me in front of the class when I made a mistake. One morning I woke up thinking, I'm going to tell my mother I have a cold and can't go to school. Much to my surprise, because I didn't feel sick, it turned out I had a fever!" Sometimes when we are feeling anxious and upset we are quite surprised to find out our bodies know all about it!

Laurie wanted to be a perfect person. She worried all the time about getting A's on every homework assignment and on every test. Her mother and father couldn't believe how neat her room was. Laurie got upset if she got a single spot on her dress, and when she ripped a hole in her sweater sleeve at school, she worried about it all day. She wanted every other child in her class to like her, so she was always doing them favors and bringing them little presents. She had the feeling that nobody would love her unless she was perfect. There are some children who feel this way even though no one has ever told them this.

When she was eight years old, Laurie began getting very bad stomach cramps and diarrhea. At first her parents thought that maybe she had eaten something that didn't agree with her, or that she had a virus. But when Laurie wasn't any better two weeks later, they took her to the doctor. After many tests and examinations, Laurie and her parents were told that trying to be perfect was causing a great deal of stress to Laurie's body. Laurie had a psychosomatic illness; her feelings were hurting her body. Laurie went to a mental health clinic where a child psychiatrist (a doctor who helps people understand their feelings) talked to her. Together they tried to find out why Laurie felt she needed to be perfect.

"Laurie," the doctor said, "your parents don't expect you to be perfect and your teachers don't expect you to be perfect and nobody can be loved by everyone. You are just the kind of person who worries a lot about these things; you were probably born like that. But now you have to help yourself by realizing you are being too hard on yourself and it is hurting your body. What we need to do together is to help you relax and to learn that all people make mistakes and fail sometimes, and that's not such a terrible thing at all."

Everything that happens to us happens to a whole person. Sometimes people may have an inherited tendency to get some particular illness. Many people who are related to each other seem to get the same illnesses, like allergies. Sometimes we get sick from poisons in the air or water, or from too many of the wrong kinds of chemicals in our food, or from eating foods to which we may be allergic. Sometimes we catch a disease like chicken pox from a friend. Sometimes when we are very angry or afraid or worried, our feelings can make our bodies get sick. There is always a combination of reasons why a person gets sick.

In recent years scientists have been figuring out something very important. What they have been studying is the immune system. When we get sick there is a system inside us that fights to make us well. It works the other way around, too. Sometimes the immune system gets knocked out of order and isn't working right. That's when we get sick.

Many things can stop the immune system from being able to protect us. Viruses and poisons or not eating properly or not getting enough exercise or smoking are a few examples. There are many things that help keep the immune system strong — mostly a healthy life. The immune system is also affected by our feelings. A person who feels sad all the time will experience changes in his or her body chemistry that can make the immune system weaker.

You may have noticed something about the immune system in school. Your best friend comes to school sneezing and coughing, and before the teacher sends her to the nurse, you and the person at the desk on the other side of your friend know that you might very easily catch that cold. For the next few days you wait to see if you are going to get a cold, but you don't. The person on the other side gets a very bad cold. When you mention this to your mother she might say, "Well, Kim has been a very upset child — she was probably run-down because of her parents' separating. That can make a person more likely to get sick."

Everything that happens to a whole human being is important when we get sick. We have known for

some time that being near someone with the kind
of illness you can catch can make you sick. We know
that people can have a special kind of tendency, like
getting hay fever because their father gets hay fever.
In recent years we have been learning that feelings
play an important part in getting sick or being well.
Doctors are not sure just how this happens — human beings are so very complicated — but we do
know that worry and unhappiness and feelings of
anger can, in some circumstances, make a person
get sick.

Just because feelings can influence illnesses doesn't
mean that a person is responsible for what happens.
We can't make feelings go away just because we
want them to. And some feelings are so deep inside
we don't even know we have them. Certainly no
child is *ever* responsible for the kind of upset feelings
that can cause a parent to get very sick.

Sara was confused. Her mother had cancer. It was
so bad that she had to have chemotherapy treatments. Doctors have found certain chemicals that
attack the cancer and in many cases cause the cancer
to go away for some time or even forever. The treatments made Sara's mother very sick; she was sicker
than she'd been when she just had cancer. The reason for this is that in order to kill the cancer cells,
the drugs have to be very strong and usually have
some side effects. Some people feel very nauseated, and some people lose their hair. Sara's parents

had explained all this to her so she was prepared.

She could also understand why her mother went to a special kind of gym class where she did a lot of deep breathing; it made her more relaxed. She understood why her mother went to see a nutrition expert who could help her choose foods that would be best for her while she was being treated with the chemicals; she needed to keep up her strength and some foods helped her not to feel so nauseated. What puzzled Sara was that her mother also went to see a psychologist twice a week. "I thought psychologists helped people who are sick in their feelings, not in their bodies," Sara said. Her mother explained, "You can't always separate feelings from your body. What I'm finding out is that I was feeling very sad about some things long before I got cancer. What I didn't understand was that I really missed going to work. It's possible that not knowing how sad I felt inside might have lowered my immune system. Also, talking about my feelings helps my body to deal with the chemicals. And talking about what I need to do to feel happier helps my immune system fight the cancer in a different way than the chemotherapy."

Sara felt very upset. "Did you get cancer from taking care of me and Danny instead of keeping your job?" Her mother hugged her tight and said, "No, no, my darling! I love you and Danny and Daddy more than anything in the world! But sometimes people decide to do something that is foolish because they worry too much about being nice and good and not listening to their inner hearts. I should have known that I could love you as much as I do, and still play the violin in an orchestra. You see, when I was a little girl I got the idea that nobody would love me unless I was a good girl and only worried about other people and never about myself. I have to learn that it's all right to love myself as well as other people. That's something I want *you* to know! But I'm sure I would be much sicker than I am, if it weren't that you and Danny make my life very important to me."

One day the psychologist came to the house when Sara's mother was feeling too sick to go to his office. When Sara let him in, she asked, "Could I talk to you for a minute after you see my mom?" It took all her courage to ask, but later on she was glad she did. The psychologist told her, "Your mother is telling you the truth. The feelings that got in the way of her immune system started many, many years before you were ever born."

Doctors, Nurses, and Hospitals

When a parent gets very sick there is a whole new world of people and places that you have to deal with — mostly doctors, nurses, and hospitals. As if it's not bad enough that you are scared because your mother or father is very sick, a hospital can sometimes make you feel worse than you already feel. For one thing, most hospitals won't let a child visit a parent. Ginny was sure her father was dying, because she couldn't see him. Her mother took her to the hospital and showed her which was her father's window, and he came to the window and waved to her, which made her feel a little better.

In the last few years many hospitals have improved the ways they can help children and families. Now they have nurses and social workers who meet with family members to help them deal with illness. Sometimes they meet with groups of children whose parents are all in the hospital. Sometimes they meet with the well parent and the children in one family. Sometimes there are discussion meetings just for the well parents. Many doctors and hospitals are finding that sick people have a better chance of getting well if they feel that someone is helping the family deal with this crisis.

Many hospitals are now realizing that although it might not be safe to let young children visit because they might be getting some childhood disease, it is not fair to let a child feel like an outsider. Some hospitals are now putting in closed-circuit TV so that a child can sit in the hospital lobby, look at a television screen, and talk to a parent, who also has a television screen and can see his or her children.

Sometimes a doctor or a nurse can make you feel

more worried. Andrew, because he is twelve and a half, was allowed to visit his mother's room. A lot of hospitals now let children over twelve visit. But the doctor didn't say a word to him; he made him feel as if he was invisible, and the nurse said, "Now don't get your mother upset or too tired." Andrew decided that the doctor ignored him because he didn't want to have to answer any questions, and he also decided that his mother must have told the nurse that he worried her and made her tired.

What Andrew needs to remember is that many grown-ups — not just doctors — have trouble talking to children. If he thinks about it, he will remember that his father's boss never talks to him and neither does the woman who lives next door. Maybe the doctor was just in a hurry to get to his next patient. Andrew also needs to remember that when his mother got sick, some grown-ups were wonderful and helpful in what they said to him, and others made him feel worse. Some nurses understand children and some don't.

Sherry's mother had a nurse for a few days after she came home from the hospital. Mrs. Kent was a wonderful person. She had *seven* children of her own, all grown up. One day Sherry came running in to see her mother after school. She was all out of breath and very excited. She had just been given the very best part in the Christmas pageant. When she ran up to the bed, her mother said, "Sherry,

I'm so tired, could you tell me about it some other day?" Mrs. Kent said, "Now, none of that, my lady! You just sit yourself up on these pillows and listen to your little girl. If you want to get well, you need to keep your children close. They bring life into this room!" Sherry's mother looked very startled. She smiled then and let Mrs. Kent help her to sit up. "What would I ever have done without this bossy, wonderful woman?" she said. Sherry sat on her mother's bed and her mother held her hand while she told about the tryouts for the play. Her mother said Sherry had cheered her up and made her feel much better.

Doctors and nurses and all the people who work in a hospital are just like other people everywhere. Some are very caring and understanding and some seem always to be in a hurry and act as if they can't be bothered with children. Noah told his father he hated the nurse who came to give his mother a bath and some injections every day. Noah described Miss Fredericks by saying, "She yells at me all the time and she acts as if she can't stand boys." His father laughed and said, "Noah, can you think of anyone she reminds you of?" Noah thought for a minute and then he laughed, too. "Yeah," he said, "she's just like Miss Wells, my second-grade teacher!" "And do you remember what happened?" his father asked. "Yeah," Noah answered. "I thought it was all my fault and you and Mom explained she was just a very unhappy woman who should never have become a teacher." When you are worried and upset because a parent is sick it is hard to remember that some people are nicer than others, and what happens isn't your fault.

Lois told her aunt, "That hospital is like a big factory! I hate going there. So many people and so many *machines!* All four people in Mom's room are attached to tubes, and every time I go there, Mom is all tired out from having to go for some new test. And it's so big you have to follow colored lines on the floor to figure out where to go!" Aunt Edith said, "I know exactly how you feel. Sometimes I think it was much better when hospitals were smaller and not so impersonal. But then I remind myself that the way they figured out what was the matter with your mother was with X rays and CAT scans and other marvelous new machines that help to save people's lives. Some of these new machines are so complicated and expensive that only large hospitals can afford to buy them. But I think things are going to change. People who work in hospitals are beginning to realize that the surroundings have a lot to do with a patient's getting better. Some hospitals now even let patients pick out paintings to put on the walls of their rooms! In some medical schools nurses and doctors are being trained to treat a *person,* not an illness. We must keep on using new equipment and new treatments, but we also have to let people in hospitals know that patients have a right to be treated with respect, that they have feelings, not just sick parts of their bodies."

Aunt Edith's son Neil was two years older than Lois and they were good friends as well as cousins. Neil said, "Why don't you arrange to call your mother after you finish your homework every day? And you could write her letters, too. That could help your mom remember she's a person, even when sometimes people in the hospital seem to forget."

Special Questions, Many Decisions

All kinds of important questions begin to come along when a parent is very sick. You may begin to wonder if your mother and father have enough money to pay for the doctors and the hospital. Before Brian's mother got sick, he had been excited about going to sleep-away camp for the first time. He felt ashamed to be thinking about that when his mother was so sick. We never have to be ashamed of our feelings, but our actions are what is really important. In spite of feeling very disappointed, Brian told his father it was all right if he needed the camp money. His father's eyes filled with tears. "What a generous and thoughtful boy you are!" his father said. "But I think we can still manage camp. What we will have to cut down on a lot is things like eating in restaurants and going to movies and ball games. Mom and I want you to have things that are really important to you, like camp, but all of us can get along without some things." Brian was so relieved about camp that he felt a wave of loving feelings for his parents. "I'm eleven years old now," he said. "I could mow people's lawns and baby-sit with Chris when you go to the hospital. We don't need to have Mrs. Reardon come anymore." His father said, "I think that's wonderful. If you could earn some money to help pay for the new clothes you'll need for school next fall, that would be a terrific help." It is natural to feel disappointed, even angry, if a parent's illness means that you can't have all the things you'd like to have. But when you help in whatever way you can, that makes you feel proud of yourself and eases some of the other feelings.

Joanne was complaining a lot to her grandmother. It is normal for a child to feel sorry for herself. The feelings are natural, but that doesn't mean we can't do anything about it. Joanne said, "Nothing is the same, everything is changing. Mom says I can't have a new dress for Wendy's party and everbody is too busy to listen to me and sometimes I feel like just running away." "It's a very upsetting time," Grandma agreed, "but you are ten years old, not a little baby. It will make you feel much better and not so sorry for yourself if you try to help. Why don't I come here a few days after school and teach you how to make caramel custard for your father? Boy, would that cheer him up, and you would feel better, too, if you knew you were doing something to make him happy."

One thing that often happens when a parent first gets sick is that the well parent and other relatives may decide that a child should be sent away for a while. The afternoon that her mother was rushed to the hospital with double pneumonia, Annie came home from school to discover that her grandmother had already packed Annie's suitcase, and was ready to rush her out of the house into the car. Annie was so scared her legs were shaking, and she was very angry, too. She felt as if she was a puppet and Grandma was pulling the strings. Grandma had forgotten to pack her teddy bear, and at least she let Annie run back into the house to get it. Grandma said, "You and I and Uncle Herbert are going to the pancake house for supper since I know that's what you love best, and tomorrow you can skip school and you'll stay with us all weekend, so your father can spend as much time as possible with your mother."

In fact, Annie always had a lot of fun with Uncle Herbert, who was much younger than her mother, but she was very upset that nobody told her what was going to happen. And being far away from home made her much more upset about her mother's being sick. It is very hard to have things done to you without your having anything to say about it. Annie might have felt better about what happened if she had told her grandmother and her father that they should have talked to her about going away from home before she went to school that morning.

Many children find they're not sure *how* they feel. When something scary is going on at home it is natural to have the feeling that you want to run away, get out of the house where people are worried and aren't paying much attention to you. The other side of that feeling, which can happen at exactly the same time, is that you need to be at home with your own belongings and in your own bed, and where you can feel part of what's going on.

It was summertime when Max's father got sick. The house was very quiet and his mother was busy taking care of his father. There was nobody to drive him places, and while some of his friends' parents picked him up sometimes to go to the pool or a movie, he was getting very bored and lonely. He kept wishing he could find a way to go somewhere, but he felt guilty about even thinking of leaving his family when his father was so sick. He felt even more guilty when his aunt and uncle asked if he'd like to go camping with them and his two cousins for two weeks. At first he felt like jumping for joy, and then he felt ashamed of himself. His mother said, "Max, darling, you've been a good sport being quiet and not being able to go anywhere. Daddy and I would feel much, much better if we knew you were having some fun." For Max, getting away from home for a while was a great relief.

When a child has mixed-up feelings, sometimes it's a good idea to make an experiment. When Sylvia's grandmother and grandfather invited her to stay with them for the whole Christmas holiday, Sylvia asked them if she could try it out for a weekend, and see how it felt. "As a matter of fact that's a good idea," Grandma said. "We know how it hurts that there won't be a Christmas at your house this year while your Daddy is in the hospital. We'll let *you* decide." Sylvia felt lonesome and sad for part of the weekend, but her grandparents took her to the ballet and they went to see the big Christmas tree at Rockefeller Center, and lots of other relatives brought their children to a breakfast party on Sunday that Grandma called a "brunch." When it was time to go home that afternoon, Sylvia said, "I think I'd like to stay if you could just take me back home for a few hours on Christmas Day, so I could see my mother and father and give them the presents I made for them." "I have an even better idea," Grandma answered. "Your mom is all worn out from taking care of Daddy, and she needs a rest. I think what we'll try to do is convince her it would be all right to get a nurse for one day, and we'll take you home for Christmas and that night we'll bring you *and* your mother to our house overnight and the next day we'll take her back. Then if you want to, for a few days we'll take you on a little trip to a place where you could begin to learn how to ski." It was a *wonderful* plan. The best part of it was that Sylvia was allowed to help make it.

One of the most important things that you can do when a parent gets very sick is to find a person or several people who can provide help and comfort. It is much, much too hard to try to be brave all the time. Noelle ran to her next-door neighbor after her father was taken away in an ambulance. Mrs. Morgan was a warm, loving woman Noelle had known all her life. She knew Mrs. Morgan would take her in her arms and hold her tight and let her cry as long as she needed to.

Jim wasn't the kind of person who could let people know how he was feeling. He wanted someone to be close but he didn't want to talk about his mother being in a hospital because she had tried to kill herself. It was so terribly painful and frightening, and he wasn't ready to even think about it. He rode his bicycle over to his best friend's house and asked if they could play chess. His friend's father was home and said he'd watch and give them some new pointers on how to play. Jim felt calmer. After they had played chess for a few hours, Mr. West said, "Jim, any time you might want to talk about what's happening at home, I'd be glad to try to help." Jim said, "Thank you," and riding back home on his bike he thought to himself that he would like to go back and

play chess with Mr. West and maybe after a while
he would talk to him about his mother.

Some children need to be alone when something
bad happens. They feel much worse if everyone is
hovering over them. Carl said, "I couldn't stand
everybody watching me every minute, to see how
I was getting along. People were trying to hug me
all the time, and I just wasn't in the mood. When
I went to my room and closed the door, my aunt
got very nervous. She kept coming upstairs every
few minutes to see how I was. Then I said I was
going to see a friend, but instead I just took a long
walk all by myself." Each person has to figure out
what will make him or her feel better. Evelyn said,
"On different days different things made me feel
better when my mother was sick. At first I wanted
my grandparents to comfort me. A few days later I
needed to talk for a long time to my school nurse,
who was wonderful to me. Then I wanted to be with
my friends almost all the time. Then one day I wanted
to just stay in my room listening to my records."
Evelyn was able to listen to her own feelings and
that can help a great deal. Listening to our feelings
is a very brave thing to do, and it will help us to
learn to live with a sick parent.

3

Living with a Sick Parent

*Jan thought she was doing so well during her moth-*er's illness; she had been taking care of her younger sister, she had been getting cereal and milk and a banana ready for her father's breakfast, and for a whole week she hadn't cried when she went to bed at night. Then, all of a sudden, everything got worse. She began fighting with her sister and having bad dreams that frightened her and when her father asked her to do some laundry, she screamed at him. "I'm not your wife! Do it yourself!"

Jan's mother wasn't just sick for a week or two. Now she had been sick for *three months;* Jan wasn't sure her mother would ever get well again. The reason Jan exploded was that suddenly everything just seemed to be too much for her to handle.

With some illnesses, although they are shocking

at first and may involve surgery or some other dramatic treatment, a parent may get well in a short time. Other illnesses, like Jan's mother's, may not seem as terrible at first, but they go on for a very long time — even forever. These are called chronic illnesses.

Seth's mother began to fall down sometimes, and sometimes her head moved in funny ways. It turned out that she had multiple sclerosis and she would have it the rest of her life. Sometimes she seemed to be fine, just the way she had been before; other times she had a lot of trouble. Seth knew that his life would be different all the years he was growing up. Gloria's mother began to go blind and there was no cure; Arthur's father lost an arm on a machine in the factory where he worked. His father learned to get along pretty well with an artificial arm and hand (called a prosthesis) but Arthur felt very bad that his father would never be like other fathers ever again.

When Your Parent Is Sick for a Long Time

It's hard enough to live through the serious illness of a parent when the parent gets well pretty quickly. It is much, much harder to live with a parent who is going to be sick for a long, long time — maybe forever.

It is normal for you to get tired of having to help all the time; it is normal to feel angry and impatient. There are just too many new chores and you have to be quiet too much of the time. It is normal to want someone to take care of you, all the time, and not to be expected to take care of yourself or brothers or sisters — and even sometimes a parent. Lucy remembers that last time she had a toothache it was her mother who took her to the dentist and took her out for lunch afterward; now her father tells her to take the bus to the dentist's office. When Fred gets a cold, he thinks about the wonderful chicken soup his mother used to make, and how she would play Monopoly with him. Now his father leaves a sandwich and a glass of milk next to his bed, reminds him not to bother his mother, and goes off to work.

When a parent first gets sick, most of your friends seem to feel sorry for you. But later on they may act bored, and some friends even start leaving you alone. You feel embarrassed when they come to the house and see your mother lying in bed in a nightgown in the middle of the day. Many children feel ashamed of having such feelings. They can't stand seeing a parent look different or act different, and they think they must be terrible children. They are not terrible at all. It is natural to want your parents to be healthy and not make your friends afraid or disgusted.

When Jan yelled at her father that she was not his wife, what she was probably feeling was that she was a *child* and everyone seemed to be asking her to grow up too fast. When a parent is sick for a very long time, grown-ups sometimes forget that children need time to grow up. A father or mother may be working so hard to keep things going that he or she hasn't got time to remember how hard things may be for the children. Too much shopping and cooking; too much baby-sitting and doing the laundry and mowing the lawn — and what is sometimes even worse, and quite a surprise, not enough discipline.

You probably always thought it would be wonderful if nobody was telling you what to do, but when you have a sick parent, you soon find out that it can be very scary not to have anyone making you behave well. Evie shivered all the way to school because no one had told her she had to wear a sweater. Carlos rode his bicycle home from school, taking the shortcut his father had forbidden him to use. He figured since his father was too sick to notice what he was doing, he could save some time. Then an older boy stopped him in the woods and took his money and his watch and his leather jacket. Carlos cried all the way home. He felt angry that his father wasn't taking care of him.

Sometimes children get upset because people are telling them what to do every second. Jack's family had to get a homemaker to take care of the family when his mother was sick. She was a nervous woman who kept treating him like a baby. She even wanted to help him take a bath! It seemed as if every other minute he had to tell her all the things his parents allowed him to do. Sometimes grandparents also worry too much and make too much of a fuss. What usually happens when a parent is sick for a long time is that one minute you want somebody to take care of you and the next minute you wish people would leave you alone. It's a natural way to feel when life changes a whole lot.

Some children begin to do things they have never done before. Faye went into a drugstore and took some candy without paying for it. She had never done anything like that before. The store owner saw her do it, and even though she returned the candy, he called her father, who told her she couldn't watch television for one week as a punishment. The strange part of it was that even though Faye felt that it was a very severe punishment, she didn't mind too much. At least her dad had paid attention to her — something he hadn't done for quite a while. Sometimes brothers and sisters will begin to fight more often, just so the parent who isn't sick will notice them. Even an angry parent seems better than one who doesn't pay attention to you.

When You Are Hurting Too Much

If you begin to do things you never did before, like stealing or playing with matches or just having a lot of trouble doing your schoolwork, it is time to get attention in a better way. Tell one of your parents you need to talk — that you are feeling very lonely and unhappy. If you can't do this, turn to the people who helped you when you first heard your parent was sick — a neighbor, the school nurse, an aunt or grandparent. It is much better to ask for real attention than to get attention because you are already in trouble.

Yvonne began to have a lot of headaches. Her teacher said, "I wonder if you have too many worries about your mother, and maybe you feel guilty because you wish your daddy could spend more time with you. You know, it's all right to feel angry and frightened by everything that is happening. I think if you will try to figure out just how you are feeling, and if we can talk about it for a few minutes after school, maybe your headaches will go away."

Yvonne's teacher was right, but it took quite some time for Yvonne to let herself know how she was really feeling because she was ashamed of what she felt. She finally figured out that it was all right to feel angry or scared, and that helped to stop the headaches. For example, three days before Thanksgiving, Yvonne got such a bad headache that she went right to the nurse's office when she got to school. The nurse gave her an aspirin (after calling her father at his office for permission) and Yvonne went to her classroom, where the children were talking about what they would be doing and where they would be going for Thanksgiving. Yvonne began to cry and wanted to leave the room. Her teacher said, "Yvonne, we are all your friends here and we know you are having a sad time right now." She told Yvonne to come sit with her and gave her a hug. Later, when the class went out for recess, Yvonne's teacher said, "You needed to feel your sad feelings and to cry, instead of getting a headache."

Yvonne told her teacher how sad and angry she felt because this year there was no way for her to have a real family Thanksgiving. Her whole family lived too far away. Mrs. Hall said she'd like to think about this problem. Later in the week Yvonne's father said, "I got a call today from Penny's mother, asking if you could go to her house for Thanksgiving dinner! Would you like to go? Mom and I will have a quiet day together and we'd both be happy to know you are having a good time." Yvonne had the feeling that Mrs. Hall might have called Penny's parents, because she knew Penny was Yvonne's best friend. She started to say thank you, but Mrs. Hall just winked at her. It wasn't like flying to her grandparents' house, but she had a good time.

Usually if you do things you don't ordinarily do,

or if you feel very scared, it means there is a feeling deep inside that you don't want to know about because you think it is a "bad" feeling. The truth is there is no such thing as a "bad" feeling. All feelings are normal. What we need to remember is that feelings don't have to lead to actions. What you might say to yourself is, "Maybe I'm feeling angry. That's an OK feeling. I need to tell someone, now that I have told myself. I could probably tell my sister or my best friend or my aunt. But best of all, I told myself, and nothing terrible happened."

Sometimes you can help get a feeling out in the open by hitting a ball in a baseball field, or pounding a pillow, or painting some kind of wild picture in school — with lots of red and black paint. Sometimes it helps to tell your troubles to your favorite stuffed animal or to punch a punching bag. Sometimes angry and scared feelings can be expressed by using up a lot of energy, going for a swim or running fast or doing some of the exercises you are learning in gym class. Sometimes letting your feelings out can make you want to do something terrific like cooking supper or baking a cake or painting a fence. We need to realize that when we are most upset it is usually because we are not allowing ourselves to feel feelings that we are ashamed of. Most often this feeling is anger. It can only hurt you if you try to push it away; it can only hurt others if you show it in hurtful ways, such as hitting. When you learn to feel your anger and to talk about it, you won't be so frightened of it. Trying to be good all the time and never complaining, even to yourself, is a burden that is too heavy to bear.

When Margo's aunt Elaine said, "It must be very hard for you to have to do so many things for yourself," Margo felt like going into her mother's room and asking if there was anything she could do. Just being told that her aunt understood her feelings made Margo feel stronger and happier. You need to learn to be your own friend just as Aunt Elaine was Margo's friend. You need to say to yourself, "This is a hard time for me and it upsets me a lot." Keeping a "stiff upper lip," keeping feelings all bottled up, is too hard. Feelings become easier to deal with when we know about them.

One of the hardest things about having a parent who is sick for a long time is that you have to learn to live with worrying for a long time. Worrying for a few weeks doesn't seem so bad when you find yourself worrying for many months or years. Once you know that a parent is going to be sick for quite some time, you need to find ways to live with worried feelings. One of the best ways is to *do* things. Worrying is a kind of feeling helpless — you feel there is nothing you can do. Worried feelings seem to go away at least some of the time if you paint a picture for your mother's room, or if you knit her a warm shawl or crochet some booties, or pick some

wildflowers and put them in a vase. Helping the
well parent can also make you spend less time worrying. You might ask if you could help to write thank-
you letters to people who sent get-well cards. You
might offer to clean out all the junk in the garage.
You might rake leaves or offer to help paint the
kitchen. Doing something helpful and useful makes
us feel that we are able to deal with our problems.
Even deciding on your own to call your grandmother
to ask her to take you shopping for clothes may be
a help to your parents, and will make you feel less
helpless.

Things That Can Help You Stay Close to a Sick Parent

When a parent is sick for a long time, you may
begin to get strange feelings about your mother and
father. Leon said, "My father stopped looking like
my father. He got very thin and his skin was sort
of yellowish. When he wanted me to hug him, I felt
funny." Probably what Leon was feeling was fear as
well as disgust. His father's hand felt funny; it was
like hugging a skeleton.

Children usually feel guilty when a parent changes
so much in appearance that it is hard to touch them.
Sheila said, "My mother loves me to hold her hand
and sit on her bed, but she scares me because she
looks so sick. Her face is all swollen. What I try

hard to do is tell myself over and over again, inside this sick body my mother is the same as she always was and wants to show me how much she loves me. My father said that if I tried, after a while I'd stop thinking about how she looked, and he was right."

Cynthia told her pediatrician, "I can't stand being near my mother. She has a funny smell that makes me feel like throwing up. I just don't feel as if she's my mother anymore." Dr. Sandor told Cynthia, "I understand how you feel. Your mother's doctors are doing everything they can to control that odor. But hard as it is for you to understand this, inside that person who seems like a stranger is *exactly the same woman* you have always known. If you look into her eyes you will see her love for you."

Erica told her father, "I've been saying 'How do you feel?' to Mom every morning for five months. I don't know what else to say, but it seems so silly." Her father said, "Mom knows that what you mean is that you love her and care about her. Could you say that, instead? Just 'Mom, I love you'? Or, 'I hope you slept better last night'?"

Erica was probably picking up a message from the way her mother looked at her every morning. On the one hand, her mother understood that Erica loved her, but on the other hand, people who are sick for a long time frequently get very tired of having other people ask how they feel. If they didn't feel pretty awful, they would be well! And no parent wants to be reminded constantly that he or she is an invalid. You can help a lot by talking about the normal things that are happening to you. Even when a parent is sick, he or she almost always is interested in seeing your homework papers, or talking about what you are discussing in your current-events class. Unless a parent is really too sick to pay attention, he or she really wants you to ask for advice and discuss your problems. When you do this your dad or mom feels like the individual he or she is, not like just a sick person.

The reason for trying to stay close to a sick parent is that this is one way in which you can help your parent get better or at least feel better.'One of the things that happens to people who are sick for a long time is that they begin to lose touch with the person inside themselves. A parent wonders, "Am I still a wife and a mother? Am I still the person who used to go to the office every day? Do other people still know me? Do I know myself?" These are called questions about *identity*. We all get certain feelings about how we look and what we know and how we feel and how we act. Being sick can make it very hard for a person to remember all this. When a child stays close and talks about everyday happenings, that helps a parent feel like him- or herself.

Chances are that if you got a very bad virus and felt very, very sick for a few days and couldn't do any of the things you ordinarily do, you might feel angry and frustrated. You wouldn't be the person you usually are. You can probably imagine how much harder it must be for someone who is sick for a long time. Your father doesn't feel like the worker he was; he used to think of himself as "Lewis, the postman." He doesn't feel much like a husband now; he used to like to take care of your mother, and now she has to take care of him. He may not even feel much like a parent now; he used to sit down with you almost every night and go over your homework and he used to take you fishing and he used to help you practice hitting baseballs.

You can help a lot. Jerry said, "I ask my mother to help me with hard math problems because she's an accountant and understands all that stuff." Donald tells his father, "We can't play baseball together, but we could watch a baseball game together on television." Another way to help a parent still feel like a parent is to go on asking the sick parent about things you want to do. Kerry got into the habit of asking her father about everything, until her mother said, "Kerry, I'm still your mother, and I can talk to you, too, you know!" Kerry began asking her mother which skirt matched which blouse; she asked her mother instead of her father if she could sleep over at a friend's house. She asked her mother if she could have an ice-cream cone after school. Her mother always smiled happily whenever Kerry asked her advice.

Sometimes a sick parent not only looks different but acts different. Some illnesses, as well as some medications, can change a person's personality. A mother seems sleepy all the time; a father forgets all kinds of things; a parent mumbles and moans a lot, or keeps shaking his head. One day a mother is friendly and wants to talk; the next day she may just stare at you and then turn away.

Such things are very, very frightening. The best thing to do right away is to turn once again to whoever you may have chosen to help you and to find out what is happening. Is it the illness? Is it drugs? Will the changes go away? What is the best way to act when a parent seems to behave in strange ways? You may need to ask your well parent to help you. This may be a period when you need to spend more time at a friend's house or visit your grandparents. Some problems are just too big for a child to live with all the time. It is not selfish to need some escape from something that is very painful.

In most chronic illnesses there are good and bad days, and good and bad times in any one day. It may help to figure out what is the best time of day to visit with a parent. Joe asked his father, "Should I talk to you before I go to school or when I get home?" His father answered, "I usually feel better early in the morning."

Some parents who are very ill aren't at home, but in a hospital or nursing home. Sometimes the place that can give the best possible care may even be in another city, so that the separation is complete. You may miss your parent far more when that happens, but in some ways it is easier than having a sick parent at home. You can get into a regular routine, you don't have to worry about making noise, you aren't upset all the time by seeing a parent who looks and feels sick. But it is important to both you and your sick mom or dad to keep in touch. You can write letters, make tapes, talk to your mom or dad on the phone, make presents to send. It is even more important when a parent is away to find other people who can help you.

When Your Well Parent Changes

Life has changed not only because of the parent who is sick. The well parent changes, too. There may be much less time to spend together; a parent may be frightened and worried much of the time, too; a parent who has to take care of everything is likely to be tired a lot of the time. It is very hard to have two parents who no longer take care of you as much as they used to. Sometimes it may be necessary to tell the well parent how you are feeling. Leslie told her father, "I'm sorry, Daddy, but I *really, really* want you to come to Parents' Visiting Day in school. I know how busy and tired you are, with Mommy in the hospital, but I feel very upset, too, and if you don't come it will be so awful for me." In most cases a parent will probably be glad to be reminded that children still need attention. Leslie's father said, "You know what, Leslie? I need to go with you for myself, not just for you. I need to spend more time with you because I need to have a little fun myself."

When a parent is sick for a long time it seems to change everything. Instead of feeling that your parents bother you too much, you feel lonely for their attention. Holidays and vacations may be canceled. Your family may have to worry more than ever before about money. Tony said, "It was bad enough when Dad told me I wouldn't get a ten-speed bike for Christmas; a few months later I was worrying about whether or not we would have enough to eat, or whether my father could pay the rent." Such thoughts can be very frightening, but it is important to remember that no matter how bad things are, you will not be allowed to go hungry or have no place to live. Sometimes relatives and friends can help; other times your father or mother might get a loan from a bank. There are social agencies that help people in trouble, ones like Cancer Care, or the National Multiple Sclerosis Society or the American Heart Association.* When things are very bad, parents may get help from the Welfare Department and from food

* Others are listed in the back of this book.

stamps. Instead of having your main meal at night at home, you may begin to have a hot lunch at school. Grown-ups are never going to forget about you. When you begin to have these kinds of fears it is very important to talk them over with one of the people you have felt comfortable telling your troubles to.

Families Continue to Change

One of the most important things for you and your family to remember is that life goes on. You will continue to grow and change. Life with a sick parent is not a make-believe life, almost like a bad dream from which you will wake up. Peggy was eight years old when her father got sick. He was still sick when she was eleven years old. Her schoolwork got harder each year, her friends changed, she grew four inches, her body was beginning to change from that of a young girl to that of a young woman. Peggy said, "When my father got sick, I never thought about what would happen if he stayed sick for a long time. Now I realize it's something that is just part of our family."

Peggy and her two brothers and her parents became closer than they had ever been before. They spent more time having family meetings so they would make plans. They had Sunday night picnic suppers right on their father's bed, every week. Peggy's father talked quite a lot about how precious life was and how he wanted his children to make the most they could of all their interests and talents. When a bad thing like a long illness happens to a family it can make people all scattered apart, and strangers to each other, or it can knit them more closely together than ever before. Jamie said, "Before my mom got sick, we never talked much about our feelings. Now we sometimes cry together, and we talk about feeling impatient or sad or worried or angry. I feel closer to my parents than I ever did before. And I feel very proud because I think we all got braver together."

Serious family problems sometimes cause people to move away from each other, and that makes everything worse. If you feel this happening in your family, you could remind your parents that you need to feel closer to them now, more than ever before. Michael told his father, "The nurse at school told me that it helps people to get better if the whole family gets together and does something they always liked to do." Michael's father paid attention to what Michael was saying. The next day, after supper, there was a family discussion in his mother's bedroom about things the family could still do together, like watching some television shows they all loved, and playing records and singing. Michael's father said, "You know, Michael, you reminded me of something I used to enjoy when I was a kid. My father loved poetry and he used to read some to us once in a while in the evenings. Maybe we could try that."

One family decided to write a family newspaper called "The Bed Post." Each day the two sisters and their brother brought stories they had written to their mother, and their father wrote a column about what was going on in the family, and sometimes one person would bring a funny article from a newspaper, or make a cartoon or write down a joke. Mother put all this together, and once a week the whole family got together at the foot of her bed, and either she or their father read the newspaper out loud.

Polly took all the recipes her mother had on scraps of paper, or torn out of magazines, and put them on three-by-five cards in a file box that she had decorated. She gave the box to her mother, saying that now it would be easier for her mother to teach Polly how to cook, when she got better. Bob got a flower box to put on the windowsill in his father's room and planted orange and grapefruit seeds, so they could watch what kinds of plants appeared. The more you do to help your family become closer than ever before, the stronger you will feel.

Of course every family is different — different people with different family histories — and that influences how families deal with serious problems. Sometimes before we can look ahead, we need to take a look backward. When we figure out the past it can help us to deal with the present and the future.

4

Things That Happened Before a Parent Got Sick

Long before Ben's father got sick, Ben was very worried about his mother and father because they often had terrible fights. Sometimes Ben would be lying in bed at night and he would hear his mother screaming, "What do you think I am, your slave? Do your own laundry — I have a job, too, you know, and if you earned enough money, I wouldn't have to be killing myself!" And then his father might get so mad he'd throw a plate across the room — Ben could hear china breaking, and his father would say, "You're a damn slob and you always were!" Sometimes even when he was in the same room they would yell about hating each other, and each one would threaten to get a divorce and leave. Ben was scared and unhappy most of the time. He never

67

knew what might happen next. Sometimes he'd come home from school and his parents would be all lovey-dovey, hugging and kissing, and other times it would sound as if a war had started. And then, suddenly, his father got very sick.

When a parent gets sick it doesn't happen in an empty space; it happens to a family, to individual people with both happy and sad stories in the background. For Ben, it was almost a relief when his father got sick because his parents stopped fighting. As a matter of fact, what he found out was that they seemed to care a lot about each other. When he saw his mother crying in the kitchen one day, he said, "I guess you don't hate Daddy anymore." His mother looked surprised. She said, "You mean because we used to argue a lot? That didn't mean anything — we're just very hot-tempered people." Ben wished someone had explained that to him a long time ago.

In Dorothy's house it was different. She and her brother, Eric, had known for more than a year that their parents were unhappy and were talking about getting a divorce; their parents were very quiet and hardly talked to each other at all. When Dorothy told Eric she felt as if she was living in some kind of desert, he said he felt that way, too. Nothing really changed very much between their parents when their mother got sick. Nurses came to take care of their mother; their grandmother moved into the guest room. Their father was almost never home.

They heard their mother and grandmother talking about moving into an apartment together after she got better. Dorothy and Eric sometimes didn't know which they worried about more — their mother dying or their parents getting a divorce.

One day Dorothy's teacher said he was very sorry to hear that her mother was sick. Dorothy started to cry and told Mr. Greenberg all the things that were happening. Mr. Greenberg said, "I think you and I and Eric should talk to Mrs. Hennessy, the school guidance counselor, about this." Mrs. Hennessy said, "I'm going to call your dad and see if he will come in and talk to me. There is a wonderful place in this city called the Crisis Center, and it sounds to me as if your whole family needs some help."

Eventually Dorothy and Eric's parents did get a divorce, but by the time this happened Dorothy and Eric felt strong enough to get through their sad and frightened and angry feelings because of the discussions they had been part of at the Crisis Center. They realized that they had thought that their mother's getting sick would fix things up with their father, but their father finally told them that for a long time he had wanted to marry someone else. It was a terrible time — worrying about their mother, being mad at their father, and wondering what was going to happen to them. Dorothy was glad that she had started to cry when Mr. Greenberg asked her about her mother. Otherwise, she and her whole family might never have gotten the help they needed.

It is hard enough for a child to handle all the feelings that come when a parent gets sick. When there are extra problems, you need to let people know, just as Dorothy did, that you need help.

There are many different family problems that may have been going on long before a parent gets sick. Judy was very scared when her mother had to go to the hospital, because her father often tried to hit her and her mother was the one who stopped him from really hurting her. Sometimes he'd even hit her mother and Judy wondered if that was what had made her mother sick. Nobody else knew about her father's having such a terrible temper; when other people were around he acted very polite and kind. As a matter of fact, Judy's mother should have told somebody about what was happening long before she got sick. But now that Judy is living alone with her father she surely *must not* keep this secret any longer. She needs to tell a person whom she trusts and who she knows will help her. People who beat up other people are sick in their feelings. Judy's father needs help as much as her mother does.

Special Decisions

Another time when children need to speak up about their troubles is when their family begins to fight about who should take care of the children. Eunice's father never got along with his mother-in-law and father-in-law. When her mother got sick, and it seemed as if she might die, Grandma and Grandpa got a lawyer and started trying to get custody of Eunice. They had been very much against their daughter's marrying John because he was Jewish and they were Catholic. They were genuinely frightened that their grandchild wasn't being raised to be a Catholic, and now they felt they had a chance to "save" her. They didn't like her father because he had long hair and a beard and played in a rock band, and traveled a lot. They also didn't like him because he was more of a pal than a father and wasn't teaching Eunice to be neat and polite.

The truth was that Eunice and her mother were both crazy about Eunice's father; he made them both feel happy. Eunice knew her father loved her a lot, even if he wasn't exactly like the other fathers she knew. She was scared when her mother got sick. Now she was doubly scared that her grandparents, whom she also loved, would take her away from her father. She knew all this was going on, but she was afraid to say anything. One day her father's sister came to see her. Aunt Frances said, "Listen, honey, you have to let your grandparents know how much you love your daddy, and that you want to stay with him, no matter what happens, even if he has to leave you with a sitter quite often. You might even have to tell a judge how you feel. You need to be very brave or nobody will know how you feel." Eunice finally got up enough courage. She told her grandparents she loved them a lot, but she loved her father even more, and that he was a very good father and a wonderful man. Her grandparents realized that there was nothing they could do because Eunice was eleven years old and they knew a judge would care a great deal about Eunice's wishes.

It can work the other way, too. Peter's father had to go to a mental hospital because he was very sick in his feelings. Before that his father had been the one who took care of Peter most of the time, because his mother never seemed to have enough energy. Grandma came to visit while Peter's father was away, and found out that Peter wasn't going to school all the time and his mother wasn't bothering to feed him properly. He was very thin and had no clean clothes and told his grandmother he was hungry. Grandma wanted to take him to her house. Peter loved his mother and was afraid to leave her alone because she really needed someone to take care of her, but he was also relieved. He knew he needed grown-ups to take care of him. Grandma called the Department of Welfare and a social worker came to visit Peter's house. She told Peter that she would see to it that his mother was taken care of. Peter went to live with his grandmother for two years. After that his father felt fine, and his mother was getting along much better and he was able to go back and live with them. Sometimes a child really wants to stay with someone else when parents just can't take care of him.

When There Is Only One Parent

One thing more frightening than having one of your parents get sick is when it is your *only* parent who is ill. Melanie's father had died just a year before they found a lump in her mother's breast and had to operate. Although everyone told her — and it was almost certainly true — that her mother would not die, all Melanie could think about was what would happen to her if her mother *did* die. As a matter of fact, that was a worry she had had ever since her father died. She knew perfectly well that a nine-year-old girl can't take care of herself.

When Melanie's mother was in the hospital, Melanie stayed with a neighbor who was also her best friend's mother. One night when Melanie had a bad dream and started crying in her sleep, Mrs. Columbo came and sat on her bed. She asked Melanie to make a list of all the people who loved her and would never, ever leave her alone. There were uncles and aunts and grandparents and friends of her mother's — quite a long list. Mrs. Columbo hugged Melanie and said, "I know your mama is going to be all right, but even if you didn't have twelve peo-

ple in your family who love you, do you think I
would ever let anything bad happen to you? Your
mama is my dear friend, and I love you, too."

When Parents Are Separated or Divorced

Vincent and his brother, Warren, lived with a
single parent because their parents were divorced.
They lived with their father on a farm in North
Carolina, and their mother lived in California with
her new husband. One day their father got hurt
when something went wrong with the threshing machine. He was rushed to the hospital. There was a
housekeeper who took care of them, but they wondered what would happen to them if their father
couldn't work on the farm anymore. Vincent, who
was older, remembered how their mother had just
picked herself up and run away, when he was four
years old and Warren was two. She wrote them
letters sometimes, but they hadn't seen her for five
years. Vincent was sure she wouldn't want to take
care of them.

When it turned out that their father's leg couldn't
be saved, Vincent and Warren were terrified. They
called their mother and told her what had happened.
She sounded really upset. She said she would come
to take care of them if that was what their father
wanted her to do, but she thought the boys should

wait until he came home from the hospital to see how he felt. Vincent had always blamed his mother for leaving him, and had always been very angry at her. After talking to her on the telephone he wasn't so sure it had all been her fault. She said, "I really do want to see you, and I've been saving money so you could come and visit me in the summertime when you are big enough to travel alone on a plane."

Vincent couldn't understand why his father had to stay in the hospital for such a long time. When he talked to his father on the telephone his father said, "Please be patient, Vincent. When I come home I'll have a surprise for you." When he did come home, he was *walking*. The reason he had stayed in the hospital so long was that he was learning to walk with an artificial leg. He told his sons that he was going to sell the farm and he had already arranged to work for a bank. He was not unhappy about this change because he felt he could be helpful to other farmers since he would understand their problems.

Warren told their father that he and Vincent had called their mother. At first their father seemed angry, but then he said he could understand that they were frightened. Vincent could tell from the way his father looked and the tone of his voice that his father didn't like their mother at all. He wondered if that was why she had run away. Vincent realized that his father's accident had helped him to see that grown-ups are so complicated that it may not be a good idea to decide who is to blame for the things that happen. When one parent gets sick or hurt, children can begin to understand parents better than they did before.

Sometimes if parents are divorced, the parent who doesn't live with the children may come back. While Marsha's mother was in the hospital, her father came to stay at the house so she could continue to go to school. Marsha kept hoping that her father would decide to come back for good after her mother came home. He seemed to be really upset that Marsha's mother was sick. Marsha talked to him about how wonderful her mother was, and how Marsha was so much happier when they all lived together. Her father said, "I'm sorry, Peaches, but Mom and I really needed to get a divorce. We like each other, but we don't love each other, and we get along much better when we don't live together. I know you're hoping I'll stay here, but neither your mother nor I can do that. When she gets home, you'll still visit me every weekend and for a month every summer, just like before." "Suppose Mom dies?" Marsha asked. That was the question that had been on her mind most of all. Her father said, "Then of course you will come to live with me." Marsha was sorry her parents weren't going to get back together, but she was relieved to know her father would always be her father.

There is something else that can be very frightening when the only parent you live with gets very sick. Jamal and his four brothers — all older than he — didn't even remember their father. He had deserted their mother soon after Jamal was born. His mother worked terribly hard to take care of her children, until she just wore herself out and became very sick. The doctor said she had tuberculosis and would need to go to a nursing home for a long time. Jamal knew that none of his relatives could take care of four boys. His aunts and his grandmother were very poor and had to work all the time just as his mother had; they had families of their own to take care of. Jamal knew some children in his neighborhood who had been sent to a foster home, and he thought that was like going to a prison. He was afraid he would be separated from his brothers and sent to a different foster home where maybe the people might be very mean. He had heard stories of children being hit and not getting enough to eat. When a social worker came to visit while his aunt was staying at his house, he almost decided to run away. The social worker told him that sometimes bad things did happen, but she had found a foster home where he could be with three of his brothers. His oldest brother was almost seventeen and he was going to live in a place where there were just older children who had almost finished high school, but he would be near enough to visit Jamal. The social worker took Jamal and his brothers to a big house outside the city, where there was a big yard, and a couple who looked like grandparents. They told Jamal and his brothers that all their children had grown up and moved away and they missed having children around the house. Jamal was scared and lonely and homesick for a while. He and his brothers hardly talked at all, and Jamal got a very bad report card. He felt so strange in a new school and he didn't have any friends. After about six months he began to feel better. Even after his mother got well, about a year later, and he went back home, he still visited his foster parents; he felt as if he had gotten two new grandparents whom he would always visit.

Jamal and his brothers were lucky that they were kept together and that his foster home was a happy place. Sometimes things don't work out so well. Timmy was placed in a foster home where there were seven other foster children. His foster mother was really mean to the smaller children. When they cried, she hit them. When Timmy took a bath his foster mother insisted on washing him, all over, and she acted very funny. Timmy knew there was something very wrong about this foster home. The next time the social worker came to visit, Timmy ran out to her car and said he had to talk to her privately and told her what was happening. He was scared because he could see the foster mother watching at the window. He did a very brave thing, and he and the other children were taken to a different home that very day. It is absolutely necessary for a child to tell someone when bad things are happening.

In most cases children who live with a single parent are either taken care of in their own homes or stay with a relative or family friends. Roy's mother belonged to a group called Parents Without Partners. Roy had gone on picnics with this group, and they had had a birthday party for him, and his mother went to meetings and parties with the people she had met. When Roy's mother got sick, all these friends arranged to take care of him. They got a homemaker from Cancer Care to stay with him, and they took him out with them on weekends, and one of his mother's friends came to see him in the school play.

Only Children and Sisters and Brothers

Even in families where there are two parents who are happy with each other, certain situations can make a parent's illness especially hard. For example, Ted was an only child. Before his mother got sick, Ted's parents went out of their way to have his friends come and visit, often overnight, so Ted wouldn't be lonely. They took Ted's friends with them when they went on vacation trips, too. Once his mother got sick, all this changed. Ted was alone so much that he got even more upset about his mother's being sick than he would have been if he had had brothers or sisters or friends to play with after school and on weekends.

Ted began to be afraid to walk home from school alone; he felt as if something terrible might happen to him. Then he began to be afraid to go to school altogether. He felt as if he wanted to cry all the time, but he tried not to. Then he began to stutter — he just couldn't seem to get the words out. What he really wanted to say was that he was angry because he was alone so much. His teacher called his father and asked if he could come in to talk about Ted. His teacher said she was very worried about Ted's being alone for a long time after school and even on the weekends when his father was at the hospital. When Ted's father came home, he said, "I'm sorry you are feeling so alone and I'm going to see what can be done about it. First of all, we're going to go out to a restaurant for pancakes on Sunday morning, and I'm going to try to spend more time with you in the evenings. Maybe we can go to a movie on Friday night. The next thing I'm going to do is talk to Aunt Kate and see if you can visit your cousins sometimes, and then I wonder whether it might not be a good idea for you to join one of the after-school recreation groups they have at the YMCA."

Ted thought that if he only had a brother or a sister everything would have been much easier. But there are lots of children who don't feel that way at all, at least some of the time. Madeline was twelve when her mother got sick. She has two younger brothers and a younger sister. All of a sudden Madeline found herself put in charge; *she* was supposed to make breakfast and *she* was supposed to give her five-year-old sister a bath at night, and *she* was supposed to make her brothers clean up their room. Her father expected her to come right home from school every day instead of hanging around with her friends. Madeline thought that it was bad enough that her mother was sick, and she wished she was an only child.

Kelly was six years old when her father was in a car accident. Her mother visited him at the hospital every single evening, and as soon as she left the house Kelly's two older brothers teased her and bullied her until she would start crying. When she tried to tell her mother, her mother got angry, and said, "Don't I have enough on my mind? Can't you try to get along together?" That didn't help Kelly feel better at all.

Something strange seemed to be happening in Tom's family. He has a twin brother and two older sisters, and while they used to fight sometimes when both their parents were around, the fighting seemed to be getting worse and worse after their mother went to the hospital; they seemed to be picking on each other almost all the time. Tom and Barry even got into fistfights. A woman came in every day to take care of the four children after school and to make their supper. Mrs. Santos got more and more exasperated with all the fighting. One day when Tom's two sisters started to cry after fighting about who could use the typewriter first for their homework, Mrs. Santos said, "You know what? I think you children are fighting with each other so you can end up crying. But you're not crying about the fight, you're crying because you miss your parents. You don't have to fight with each other to cry about that — you can just cry about being worried."

Sometimes brothers and sisters become closer than ever before when a parent gets sick. That seems natural and they feel good about it. Some brothers and sisters fight more than they ever did before. That's natural, too, but children usually feel guilty about that. When you are sad and frightened, you need to be comforted, and brothers and sisters can sometimes comfort each other. But it is also natural that when you are sad and frightened, you may need a "random target," which means that underneath feeling sad and frightened you probably also feel angry at what is happening. You feel you can't be angry at the parent who is sick, and you feel you can't be angry at the parent who is trying to take care of everything, and so instead you get mad at a brother or sister. You choose another target for all your angry feelings.

Sometimes a child like Madeline who is suddenly burdened with new responsibilities needs to ask for help. If her father is too upset, she might call her grandparents or an aunt or a neighbor. She might even ask her father if he would hire a baby-sitter at least one or two afternoons a week so she could be with her friends. If parents forget that you are still a child and can't become a mother or father, you might have to remind them.

Kelly needs to tell someone besides her mother, who is too upset to listen, that her brothers are making her very unhappy. Maybe her best friend's mother would let her stay at her friend's house some afternoons. Or maybe she could bring a friend home to her house; her brothers wouldn't pick on her in front of someone else. Maybe she can ask a grandparent to let her visit over a weekend by herself, to get a rest from her brothers.

It helps brothers and sisters to get along if they can talk together about how upset they are. After Mrs. Santos suggested that when Tom and his brother and sisters were fighting with each other, they were really showing how upset they felt about their mother's illness, they began to get along better. They even sat down together and talked about their worries. They talked about what would happen when their mother came home. One day Tom even said to his twin when they were lying in bed in the dark, "Do you think Mom might die?" He found out Barry was wondering about that, too, but was too scared to talk about it. They got along a whole lot better after that discussion.

Decisions About Money

There are other circumstances that influence what happens when a parent gets sick. If a family has plenty of money, that at least is one less thing to worry about. But that isn't often the case. Even a family that has had enough money to live very comfortably can get into debt very quickly, with doctor and hospital bills. And for families with very little money to begin with, a long illness can be very serious.

It also makes a difference how a family felt about money before a parent got sick. Elliot's father and mother both worked, but never made a lot of money. Whenever they had any money, they always wanted to spend it right away — they would go to a restaurant to eat when their father made a car sale, and they bought a lot of camping equipment when their mother got a raise. "Money is just for enjoying life," Elliot's father said. It was a shock to everyone when Elliot's mother got sick and they didn't have enough money to pay all the bills.

Things were very different in Lena's family. Her mother stayed at home; her father took care of everything having to do with money. He gave his wife and his children an allowance, but he wanted to know exactly how the money was spent. When Lena wanted to use part of her allowance to get something advertised on a cereal box, he wouldn't let her do it. Lena thought this was very unfair. "What's the use of my having an allowance," she asked her father, "if I can't spend it on what I want?" Her father got angry and said he worked much too hard to let anyone in the family waste money. When Lena's father got sick, the whole family fell apart. Lena's mother hadn't ever learned how to make out checks; she didn't even know which bank her husband used. Grandma and Grandpa had to come and help. When her father got sick, Lena felt as if her whole world was collapsing.

Sometimes children never think very much about money until a parent gets sick. Then it may be all that parents seem to talk about. You always had the feeling that your parents would provide a home, that they would buy food and clothes and toys and everything you ever needed. Now, all of a sudden, you don't even dare to ask for Christmas presents, and you never have steak anymore for dinner, and instead of getting new clothes when school starts, you are told you will have to wear your older sister's dresses or your older brother's sweaters.

Children worry about money and they also are likely to feel angry that they can't have the things they want. You might feel less worried and angry if

you think about ways in which you can help. Lisa
and her sister made lemonade and iced tea, rode
their bicycles to the shopping center with jars and
paper cups in the bicycle baskets, found some empty
boxes to use as tables at the big supermarket, and
sold their drinks in the parking lot. It was a hot
summer and they made enough money not to have
to ask their father for any allowance. Victor was
wonderful at fixing things like toasters and alarm
clocks. He put an ad in the local town paper, and
worked in his father's workshop in the basement. It
took a while to get started, but when people began
to realize what a great "fixer" he was, they gave him
more and more things to repair. Millie's mother had
taught Millie how to make brownies, and Millie
went from door to door in her apartment building
and sold as many as she could make on Saturday
mornings.

Some children are old enough to be baby-sitters;
others might get a newspaper route. Some can offer
to mow other people's lawns or paint fences or help
out at birthday parties for younger children. Doug-
las bought some packages of seeds in the early spring
and later on he set up a stand in front of his house
and sold the plants. When you can earn your own
spending money, or take the whole family out
for hamburgers, or buy a beautiful bed jacket for
your mother, or bring your father a new chess set
in the nursing home, you have a feeling of pride

and satisfaction that takes away some of the worrying.

Where You Live

Where you happen to live when a parent is sick can make a big difference. Naomi lives in New York City, where she always had taken a city bus to school and a subway to her piano lessons, and she can walk to her pediatrician's office. When her mother is in the hospital she can go right on doing what she has been doing all along. The situation is very different for Lester. He lives in a suburb of Cleveland. He takes a school bus to school, but his mother always had to drive him to his after-school swimming classes and to visit his friends, or to go to a movie or to the dentist. Now, while his mother is in the hospital, there is no one to drive him anywhere. He and his father have to figure out all kinds of complicated arrangements and ask other people to help.

It also makes a big difference if you have relatives who live nearby. Dennis's grandparents live in the downstairs part of his house, and two aunts and three uncles live less than five miles away. If anything, Dennis sometimes feels that too many people are taking care of him. On the other hand, Florence has only one grandmother, who lives two thousand miles away; she has no aunts and uncles, but she does have other people who care about her. The minister of her church found someone who wanted to be her make-believe grandmother. Florence was a little shy at first, but then she had fun going out with this new friend who said, "I know you don't want to call me Grandma, because that's only for your real grandmother. How about calling me Nana? That's what my grandchildren call me, but they live so far away I hardly get a chance to see them. I was feeling very lonely for them, and I'm so happy to have a make-believe granddaughter now!"

When a parent gets sick one very good thing happens: children find out how many people care about them. Nancy and her parents had just moved to San Diego from Boston a few months before her mother got sick. There hadn't been much time to make new friends, but her mother's secretary called Nancy's father and said she would like to bring over some food she had cooked that could be put in the freezer for their suppers. Her father's boss said he could leave at four o'clock instead of five until Nancy's mother got better. The lady next door said that Nancy could come to her house after school any day she wanted to. She said, "My husband died last winter and my children are grown and live far away — it would be wonderful to have you visit me."

What we all are more than likely to find out when something terrible happens is that there are many, many people who want to help. We also discover that no matter how bad things seem to be, change is taking place all the time. You are growing up; better arrangements are made for taking care of things at home; you stop thinking about your sick parent all the time and you begin to get back to doing things you did before your parent got sick.

And very often, you may find yourself surprised by the most important change of all: your mother or father gets well again!

5

When a Parent Gets Well

*When Derek's mother got sick, Derek swore to him-*self that if she would only get well, he would *never ever again* do anything to upset her. When the doctor said she was all better, Derek was shocked by how he felt. First he had a wonderful feeling of relief but then he felt very angry! He couldn't believe it. He had thought he would love his mother more than ever. But there she was, standing near the stove cooking her first dinner in three months, and it was all he could do not to scream at her. He was so scared of his terrible feelings that when she smiled and wanted to hug him he ran to his bedroom.

The way Derek felt was not so surprising. Now that his mother was safe, all his frightened feelings were surging up to the surface of his mind. He ran

out of the room because what he wanted to shout
at his mother was, "How could you have done such
a terrible thing to me? How could you get so sick
and make me so frightened?" That is a natural feeling, when we keep things bottled up inside for a
long time. It's when we feel safe again that all the
pain and worry and anger comes out all of a sudden.
Even if Derek doesn't say anything to his mother,
it is good to let such feelings come out, if only in
the privacy of his own room, because what usually
happens is that these feelings can then go away in
a short time.

Angry feelings are normal. It feels as if you went
through all that pain and suffering for nothing. It
helps to remember that it *wasn't* for nothing, because your mother or father is well again and all
that you lived through and the ways in which you
tried to help have made you a stronger person than
you were before. Probably your whole family now
feels how precious life is and how important love in
a family can be.

But that's not the whole story. What surprised Niki
was that it didn't even take a whole week before she
and her mother got into a fight about whether or not
she could wear jeans that had a hole in the knee
to school. Her mother couldn't understand that in
Niki's class at school it was considered cool to wear
jeans that didn't look too clean or new. Niki heard
herself saying, "It was better when you weren't here!

Nobody bothered me about what I wore to school!"
Then she and her mother both burst out crying, and
Niki said over and over again, "Oh, Mommy, I didn't
mean it, I didn't mean it!" Niki's mother said, "We
have to get used to me being the mother and you
being my child, all over again."

When you have had to take care of yourself part
of the time and after you have been doing some of
the jobs that your mother or father usually did, it
is not easy to give up that new independence. Sometimes it may be a good idea to say, "Mom, I really
learned to do a lot of things and I'm nine years old
now and I was only seven and a half when you got
sick, so you have to stop treating me like a baby."
Not only is it hard on you when a parent begins to
act like a parent again, but it may be very hard for
a parent who has been in a hospital or a nursing
home for a long time to recognize the changes that
have taken place while he or she has been gone.

For example, Marvin's father felt very bad and
Marvin felt guilty. What happened was that while
Marvin's father was in the hospital, his uncle Aaron
had started taking Marvin to baseball games and
spending quite a lot of time with him. They had a
special place that made the best pizza, and Marvin
had talked to his uncle about some of his friends
and his teachers and what subjects he liked in school
and what subjects he hated. When his father came
home, Marvin felt very funny. He realized that he

wanted to go talk to his uncle more than he wanted
to talk to his father. After trying to start a conver-
sation, Marvin's father said, "I seem to have lost a
son as well as a kidney! All you talk about is Uncle
Aaron this and Uncle Aaron that. You don't seem
to need me anymore!" Marvin felt terrible because
it seemed to be the truth. For several weeks he and
his father hardly talked to each other at all. Finally,
Marvin told his uncle about it. Uncle Aaron came
to the house and said he wanted to speak to Marvin's
father alone. Later Marvin's father told Marvin what
Uncle Aaron had said. "Your Uncle Aaron really told
me off!" he said. "He reminded me of how scared
and lonely you were while I was gone, and you didn't
even know for sure whether I'd ever come back. I
realize now that it was wonderful that my brother
tried to take my place. I would want to do the same
thing for his son. But I hope we can start being
friends again."

Many children feel very strange when a parent
gets well. They got used to a different kind of re-
lationship — they have often forgotten what a parent was like before the illness. Parents and children
need time to get reacquainted. You need to understand that when your parent gets well the change
and the adjustment back to the way life was before
is as big a change for everyone as it was when your
parent first got sick.

Some Surprises

Sometimes a diagnosis turns out to be wrong. For a while Evan's father's doctors thought he had liver cancer but it turned out to be hepatitis, something much less serious that they could treat. Evan felt all mixed up. He had prepared himself for something terrible and then all of a sudden, the terrible thing was gone. But, instead of feeling happy and relieved, he felt sort of depressed. The reason for this was that his mind and his body had gotten him all ready to face a disaster. And when the danger was suddenly over, he had to get himself reorganized. Suppose Evan had been awakened one night and told the house was on fire. His whole body would have set itself in motion — he would have run outside with his parents as fast as possible. If the fire had been put out very quickly without doing much damage, no one would have been able to go back to sleep right away — everyone would have felt restless and overexcited. His father might have said, "I think we all need some hot cocoa to calm down." When a parent gets well unexpectedly, it may take quite a while to calm down.

This can be especially upsetting because you probably thought that the minute your father or mother was well again, everything would be perfect. Your parents would never argue anymore, and they would never get impatient, and you would be a perfect child. Now you realize you can forget all about that dream! It just doesn't happen. Human beings may behave unusually well during a serious crisis, but when it is over we all go back to being normal people who have moods and who get tired and impatient and angry. *That* is what is normal. Now your father wants to get back to all the work he let go when your mother was sick; he comes home tired and cranky. Your mother looks at the pantry shelves and gets mad because everything is a mess; she doesn't realize what a hard job it was trying to keep things going. Your teacher gets angry because you handed in a messy paper and she says, "There's no excuse now for sloppy work; your father is all better, and I expect you to shape up," and you come home feeling tired and angry and don't want to kiss Grandma, who has come to visit. It's a shock to have everything getting to be just the same as it was before. But later on you will be glad people (including yourself) are acting like human beings, not trying to be perfect. It will be a relief not to feel you have to put on an act. It's a relief to know everyone in the family is getting back to being him- or herself, but it takes time.

Grace experienced another feeling that is quite common when children are told a parent is all well again. She said, "Now I worry all the time that it isn't really true — that my mom will get sick again." Once you have been terribly frightened, it is natural to feel that life is very uncertain, so that you can no longer count on anything. Of course it is always possible that something could happen to someone in your family in the future. But after a while you will stop thinking about this so much and if something does happen, now you know you are quite a strong person.

All human beings forget difficult times after they are over. If we always remembered how bad we felt, it would be very hard to go on with our lives. Felice was shocked that just two days after her mother came home, her mother and father were laughing while they were watching a funny television show. How could they forget so fast how awful it was, she thought to herself. She was still remembering that terrible feeling in the pit of her stomach when her father told her her mother needed to have an operation. Then, about two weeks later, she went to an overnight pajama party where she and her friends giggled almost all night long. When she went home the next day she realized she was beginning to forget the bad times, too.

There can be some wonderful changes in a family when a parent gets over being sick. Even though people go back to behaving normally, there can still be a special feeling of love. Or sometimes you feel that a great deal of stress has disappeared. Jessica said, "Before my mom got sick, something bad was going on between her and my father. I wasn't sure what it was, but I think my mother didn't like my father's new secretary, who was very young and pretty. She wanted him to fire her. I never heard another word about that after Mom was sick, even though Daddy still had the same secretary. Then one day I heard my mom talking to Grandma on the phone and she said, 'When Allen cried when I came back to my room after the operation, I realized how much he loved me. I have to get over being so stupid and jealous.' "

Sometimes, however, it can be a big shock to find out that mothers and fathers seem to have more problems after a parent gets well. They may fight and yell more than they ever did before. Often this is the same thing as a child's feeling angry when a parent is well again. They are really relieved, but all the exhaustion from worrying and having to be brave comes to the surface, and their nerves are frayed. When anyone goes through something terrible, there comes a time, once things are better, when he or she just has to let down and let go. It may be hard to get along together for a while. Unless there were serious problems long before the illness, parents calm down fairly soon.

Things That Help a Family Recover

Usually the whole family needs some relief from the strain. If your parents don't think of it first, you could suggest that this might be a good time to go on a camping trip, or to have a bigger birthday party for your mother or father than you ever had before and invite relatives from all over the country, to celebrate the good news. One father said, "I know life is uncertain and I want us to have as much fun as we can, now, not next month or next year." He and his children began taking tennis lessons, and they went to museums on weekends, and they took a ferryboat ride they had talked about for several years.

Families need to recuperate together at least some of the time. But they also need time to each have a separate life again. It would be natural if you wanted to go on a vacation trip with your grandparents. Now that the crisis is over, you just want to get away, not think about it, have a lot of fun. Harriet said, "I'm glad my father came home just before the summer, so I could go to camp for a month and just get away from the house. It helped me get over all the worries, and I needed to get away from my parents, now that everything was all right."

Tricia kept having the feeling that unless she came home right after school every day, her mother might get sick again. One day her mother asked her why she didn't talk about her friends anymore, and why none of them ever came to the house the way they used to. Her mother said, "I was trying to figure out what was different around here, and then I realized the telephone wasn't ringing all the time and you weren't glued to it every day after you'd done your homework!" Tricia said, "I thought you might need me to help you. I don't want you to get sick again!" Her mother said, "Tricia, if you really want me to feel good, you go have fun with your friends, and don't worry about me. I need time by myself and I need to see my friends again, and I want to know you are having a good time."

Sam was told that his father would have multiple sclerosis for the rest of his life. Sam had worked very hard to get used to his father's having trouble walking and falling down and shaking sometimes. What he didn't know was that in some chronic illnesses there can be long periods of remission when the illness seems to disappear for a while and the person seems all well again. When his father felt well enough to go back to work, Sam felt all mixed up. Was his father sick or was he well? Sam didn't know how to act.

What Sam needed to do was to talk to his father about how confused he was. Or he might have talked to a doctor or a nurse about what this illness is like, what was likely to happen. It is very hard to live with a parent who seems quite sick at one time, and then appears to be healthy at another time. It helps a lot if the whole family can sit down together and talk about this.

When a parent has been mentally ill and comes

back home, most children are likely to be frightened. They wonder if anything they say or do could make their parent start crying a lot again. This is a time when children need to get some help from grown-ups. They need to find the person they trust and can talk to, in order to learn as much as they can about why someone can get so upset and even act very strangely. They need to realize that children are never responsible for the emotional problems of their parents and that they do not have the power to make them sick or make them well. People who are mentally ill usually have had troubles with their feelings most of their lives. It may be that you can help at first by letting your parent get used to being home again — to go on doing things just as you were doing while he or she was away. Sometimes it takes a while to adjust to being part of a family again. But if you walk around on tiptoes, and talk in hushed whispers, that doesn't help a parent get used to being home again. The best thing you can do is to be yourself, to let your mom or dad know you feel a lot of love.

Sophie was afraid of her mother. She felt awkward and shy. For several months her mother had hardly noticed Sophie was around; she hadn't seemed to know that Sophie was her daughter. That was so frightening that when her mother came home, and held out her arms, and wanted to hug Sophie, she ran out of the house. And then she was afraid to go back home because she felt she had done something terrible. What Sophie needed to understand was that when a parent has had a mental illness, he or she has been talking to a therapist, a person who is trained to understand these kinds of problems. It's more than likely that the psychiatrist Sophie's mother saw in the hospital had said to her, "You must expect Sophie to feel uneasy with you at first. You will have to give her time to realize you are able to be her mother again."

Chances are her mother knows how Sophie's feeling, so there is no reason for Sophie to think she has to run away or feel guilty. Her feelings are natural. She also needs to understand that her mother is going to go on seeing the psychiatrist every week, and that he is going to help in every way he can. He may have given Sophie's mother some medicine to help her adjust to being back home, and these medications might make her mother seem quite sleepy sometimes, or she may seem to have more energy than she had before she got sick. Sophie might say she would like to talk to her mother's doctor, because she wants to understand what is happening. She can certainly talk to her pediatrician or family doctor or the school nurse, but what she has to remember is that she is not responsible for taking care of her mother. All she can do is to be herself — say and do the things she has always said and done. If her mother gets upset about anything that happens at home, Sophie needs to remember that her mother has a doctor to help her. In some cases a parent's doctor will want to spend some time meeting with the whole family and that can be helpful and comforting for everyone. Other times the doctor may feel this would not be good for the patient and that's when the other members of the family will need to seek help elsewhere.

One thing we learn from a parent's illness is that life changes all the time. Once a mother or father has been well for several months, it will probably be hard for anyone in the family to remember too clearly what it was like when she or he was sick. Life goes back to what it was like before the illness. But there is one big difference. Now you know that even when something terrible happens you are able to go on living.

6

If a Parent Dies

When Melinda's father died from a heart attack it came as a complete shock. Nobody had any idea that there was anything wrong with her father. Sometimes he seemed quite tired but everyone thought that was because he worked so hard. He seemed healthy and strong and he loved working outdoors — fixing the roof of the house, mowing the lawn and cutting firewood. That was how he died — chopping down a tree on a Saturday afternoon. After he died, the doctors realized he had had heart trouble for quite a long time. But for Melinda and her family, there was no preparation at all.

Sometimes, of course, a parent who has been seriously ill for a long time may die. Melinda had a friend in school, Beverly, whose father had been fighting cancer for a year. Melinda's and Beverly's fathers died within two weeks of each other. Melinda said to Beverly, "It's not so bad for you, because you knew your father might die and you had time to get used to the idea." Beverly was puzzled; could this be true? It sounded sensible, but somehow it didn't seem to have anything to do with her feelings. It seemed to Beverly that she was just as shocked as Melinda, and just as sad.

No matter how sick a parent might be, and no matter for how long, it is still a terrible shock when a parent dies. We are never really able to imagine what a death is like until it happens. There is no way in which anyone can imagine ahead of time how final a death is. The pain is just as great even if we think we have been prepared. Kevin said, "I knew how sick my mother was, and nobody lied to me. Sometimes I even went for a walk by myself and I would sit on the beach near our house, and hide in the tall grass and cry and cry, thinking about my mother dying. But when she died it was different. She wasn't in her bed, and I knew I would never see her again. It wasn't like anything I imagined."

While the pain and shock may be just as great whether a parent dies suddenly or after a long illness, there are some important differences. If you have lived through a long illness of a parent, you know some things about yourself that other children may not know. You know that you will go on living;

you know there are many people who love you and won't ever leave you alone; you know you can find the people you need to talk to; you know that angry feelings are natural; you know that you are strong enough to go on with your life. You have learned that one of the things that helps the most is letting yourself feel your feelings.

Another difference is that you have had a chance to say good-bye. All the kind and caring things you have done, all the times you held your mother's or father's hand, all the times you said "I love you" were ways of saying good-bye. It was the same for your mom or dad; the things she or he talked about, the way she or he looked at you were ways of saying good-bye.

A parent's death is the most terrible thing that can ever happen to a child. Even after a long illness and preparation it still feels like the end of the world. But you may need to remember that you felt something like that when your parent got sick. Life did go on then, and when a parent dies, you will find that life goes on then, too.

Many of the feelings you had when your parent became sick become even stronger, but now at least you know that all these feelings are normal. First there is the shock and the not believing; you feel as if it's all a terrible nightmare and soon you will wake up. And then there is the feeling that what has happened is just plain impossible; nobody so im-

portant, so special, could be gone forever. And then
there are all the fears and the anger you felt at the
very beginning.

Confusing Feelings

Matthew told his aunt Ruth, "There is something
the matter with me. I just don't feel anything at
all — I just feel numb all over." His aunt Ruth said,
"Darling, that's perfectly natural. You have been
grieving for your father for so many months that
there just aren't any more feelings left. Later on
your feelings will come back and you will feel awful
for quite some time. Right now you are exhausted
from worry and sadness."

This numbness can be true for a whole family. It
is caused by extreme exhaustion. After taking care
of her sick husband for eight months, Charlotte's
mother just sat in a chair; she couldn't talk and she
couldn't cry. "There's just nothing left inside of me,"
she said.

This lack of feeling may last for a few days or even
longer. "What happened to me," Alexis said, "was
that after the funeral I came home and went to bed
and slept for half a day, a whole night, and part of
the next morning. When I woke up my feelings
began to come back and I cried and cried. And then,
later, I remembered how my mother and I had taken
care of everything while my dad was sick. Mom had

gotten a good job and she already knew some people who wanted to buy our house, and we did all the housework together on Saturday mornings, and we had spent a lot of time with her friends and my friends and I already knew my grandparents wanted to help us. Even while I felt worse than I ever felt in my whole life, I realized I was strong and my mother was strong. My dad hadn't been doing anything with us for so long that it didn't seem strange to eat supper or go to a movie without him." When a parent has been very sick for a long time, it is natural that the other members of the family have gotten ready to live without that parent in many ways.

One of the biggest fears you may have when a parent dies is that you will forget what your mother or father looked like. In the very beginning when a person dies most people seem to have a very hard time picturing that person inside their heads. It's very frightening and upsetting. But it never stays that way. When the shock begins to wear off, we remember so many things. Sometimes we remember a father singing, or we can remember the perfume a mother wore, and soon we remember happy times and angry times and trips and holidays and we begin to look at pictures and tell stories about things that happened. What we find out as time goes by is that while we may never see a parent again, that person hasn't disappeared at all. The person lives on in our memories, and in the things he or she did while alive.

Terry has all the sweaters and hats and scarves her mother knitted for her; every day Harold sees the African violets his mother loved so much, sitting on a table near the window, and he begins to take care of them and love them as much as she did. Willie has all the stories his mother made up and illustrated herself, and he thinks that maybe someday he'll give these homemade books to a child of his own. Joyce's mother insisted on taking hundreds of pictures and there are great big fat family albums that Joyce will always have to remind her of the years when her father was alive. Justin loves to cook, and he keeps his mother's card file of all the recipes she liked the most.

Sometimes a child will try too hard to keep a memory alive. When Margaret's father died, she put dozens of his pictures all over her room. She put two candles on her dresser and in between she put her father's pipe and his favorite tie and his baseball hat. She took all the letters he had written her when he was on business trips, and tied them up with a great big red bow, and kept them next to the lamp on her bedside table. As soon as she got home from school she would begin to play her father's favorite records. Margaret was desperately trying to keep her father alive. Her mother was very worried. After a few weeks, when Margaret still didn't seem to be interested in anything except thinking and talking about her father, Margaret's mother said, "I know how much you loved Daddy, but do you think he would want you to stop seeing your friends and stop reading new books and stop taking piano lessons? Do you think he would want you to sit in your room every afternoon?" Those were good questions, and Margaret thought about them quite a lot. Slowly but surely she tried to begin to do all the things her father would have been happy to see her doing. Margaret realized that the best way to remember a parent who has died is to go on growing up in as happy a way as you can.

Different Family Customs

You already know a great deal about feelings. You also know about how different people behave in different ways. Just as one person was very helpful when your mother or father got sick, and some other people seemed to make things much worse, the same thing now happens about death.

Roger's grandmother was in the dining room, talking to his mother. She said, "You surely aren't thinking of taking Roger to the funeral and the cemetery! How could you submit a nine-year-old boy to such a terrible experience?" For a moment Roger felt frightened and lonely as he listened from the kitchen. And then he heard his mother say, "The most terrible thing has already happened to Roger. He needs to be with the people he loves and who knew Henry, just as much as I need to." Roger cried a lot at the funeral service, and he had bad dreams for a week about people in coffins being buried in the ground, but he knew that if his mother had left him home, what he imagined would have been worse than what actually happened.

One thing we have found out is that children need to be part of what happens when a parent dies. They need to know that grown-ups will answer all their questions, and that they will be able to join with all the grieving friends and relatives as much as they want to.

Children need grown-ups to help them decide just how much they want to do. In Patrick's family it is the custom to leave the coffin open until after the funeral and for people to go up and say their last good-byes. Patrick's mother asked him if he wanted to look at his father. Patrick was so scared he was shaking. His mother thought it would be good for him, but his uncle Sean said, "When Mama died, I went up to the coffin. For a long time all I could remember was that she didn't look like Mama at all — so still, almost like she was made of wax. I wish I had just remembered her in the kitchen on Christmas morning yelling at all us kids to get out of the way!" Patrick thought about what both his mother and his uncle Sean had said. Then he decided that most of all he wanted to remember his father laughing at a joke Patrick had told him when he was sick in bed. He decided not to go up to the coffin.

Benjamin's family was Jewish, but his parents never went to temple or celebrated the Jewish holidays. But Benjamin did go to Sunday school because he knew how much his grandparents wanted him to have a bar mitzvah when he was thirteen years old, and he had learned about Jewish people "sitting shiva" for one week after a person died. When his mother died, Benjamin told his father that he wanted to stay home from school and be very quiet. His grandparents said they would stay with him. His father could see how much this meant to Benjamin, and he said, "I'm going to stay at home with you." By the time Benjamin went back to school, he felt quite peaceful even with all the sadness inside him.

Children need to be part of the mourning for a parent who dies. May's mother didn't understand that, and she left May and her sister with an aunt and went away for two weeks by herself. She said she didn't want her daughters to see her crying all the time. The day she came back and held her arms out to May and her sister, they ran out of the house. Having been separated from their mother at a time when they needed to be near her the most, they now felt she was a stranger.

When children don't get the help they need from

grown-ups, they can become confused. Jennifer wasn't told anything about the baby brother who died in the hospital right after he was born. Her parents just said he was sick, but they wouldn't answer any questions about what happened after he died. Jennifer began to have terrible nightmares, all about a baby floating around the house, or hiding in a dresser drawer, or lying at the bottom of her bed.

She got so tired and scared that she said she couldn't go to school. Her parents went to see the school counselor. They told Mrs. Jacobi that they just couldn't tell Jennifer the truth because the baby had been cremated and Jennifer was too young to hear about it. Mrs. Jacobi said, "What Jennifer imagines in her dreams is much worse. You must tell her the truth." The next day Jennifer's father finally got up his courage and explained to Jennifer that there are two things that can happen when a person dies. He or she can be buried in the ground in a coffin or the body can be burned very rapidly in a special kind of oven, and then the ashes buried in a small urn like a closed vase or box. The baby's ashes had been buried under a tree in the backyard. Jennifer's father was quaking in his shoes. He was so afraid that now Jennifer would be more scared than ever. Instead, she sighed with relief. "I'm glad you told me," she said. "Now whenever I climb that tree I'll be remembering that little baby who was too sick to stay alive."

Special New Fears

A fear that all children have when they lose one parent is that they might lose the second parent. After their father died, Liz and Sue got very frightened whenever their mother had to fly to business meetings. Ronnie worried all the time because his father still went on smoking cigarettes even though everybody said it was dangerous to smoke. When Marilyn's father died, she heard her mother crying and telling Grandma, "I can't go on alone! I wish I were dead!" Marilyn wanted to scream, "And what will happen to *me* if you die, too?" In the very beginning, when a parent is suffering the most, she may say things she doesn't really mean. Marilyn's mother was expressing her grief. A week later she began to take care of Marilyn again. Chances of losing both parents are *extremely* small. But the fear is natural. After a while it comes less often. And when a parent has been sick for a long time, a child has already learned how many, many people are loving and caring and would never, ever leave a child alone.

Feeling Guilty

There is another kind of feeling that is also very normal but about which children sometimes feel very guilty. Brooke was very close to her daddy and he adored her. He used to call her "my little beauty," and even when she was getting quite big she still loved to nestle in his arms and sit on his lap. Several months after he died her mother was yelling at her one Saturday morning about cleaning up her room. Her mother shouted, "You are a slob! A filthy pig, and I can't stand it anymore!" Without thinking, Brooke said, "I wish you had died instead of Daddy!" Then she was horrified by what she had said. At first her mother looked shocked and then her eyes filled with tears. Brooke ran and hugged her and said, "I didn't mean it. I didn't mean it!" After they both calmed down Brooke's mother said, "I know you were Daddy's very special little girl and I know how much you miss him. I do, too — I guess that's why I lose my temper more often. But we both have to understand that now it is my job to help you grow up into a fine woman and sometimes I will have to scold you and punish you, and it will make you mad. But then you need to remember that Daddy wanted you to become a nice grown-up, too."

Sometimes it happens the other way around. Marc was terribly ashamed that along with all the other kinds of feelings he had when his father died, there was also a feeling of relief. His father had had a terrible temper and was often very mean to Marc's mother. Sometimes his father got so mad he packed his bag and went away for a week or longer, and sometimes he didn't even let Marc's mother know where he was. Marc sometimes heard his mother crying in the next room when he went to bed at night. Now, he thought, life will be better and calmer — and then he realized that both he and his mother would give anything just to hear his father shouting again. Such mixed-up feelings are also very natural.

If a Parent Remarries

When a parent dies, children worry a lot about whether or not their living parent will marry again. There are lots of confusing feelings about this, too. On the one hand, you think you might feel much safer if you had two parents to take care of you; on the other hand, suppose it was somebody you didn't like, or who didn't like you? And suppose this new parent had children? They might be brats. And it would be so hard to have to get to know new sets of relatives. A new parent might not let you go on remembering your mother or father as much as you need to. Sometimes a child is happy to see a parent begin to date; other times this can be very frightening. The worst fear is that your only parent may stop caring about *you,* most of all.

Difficult as it may be, children must allow a parent to make decisions about dating and marrying. These are not choices that children can make. You can certainly let your mom or dad know how you are feeling, and what may be worrying you, and you can certainly let a parent know when you like someone he or she is seeing, but all decisions should be made by the grown-ups. What you need to remember is that it takes a long, long time for new people in a family to get used to each other; it will probably feel very peculiar to have a new person sitting in the same chair where your mother or father once sat. It may make you very angry to have your mother's boyfriend bossing you around; it may be very confusing when your stepmother is fussy about things that never bothered your mother and not at all fussy about things that your mother was very strict about. It may seem at first that a new brother or sister is the worst bully or worst pest you ever met. But gradually your new family begins to develop its own special history. After a while you all remember the same trip to Disneyland; you all remember a blizzard in which you couldn't get out of the house for three days; you all remember how everyone got scared when there was a fire in the kitchen. Slowly but surely you'll get used to each other, sometimes through good and happy times, but also through times when there may be lots of anger and disappointment. The new older sister who tried to boss you around eventually becomes someone you can tell your troubles to; or you realize you must be beginning to love that new little brother when you worry because he has to have his tonsils out. For a long time it made you really mad to see that your mother could be happy and in love again — and then your stepfather helps you build a tree house, and you realize he really cares about you, too.

It can help to remember that families never happen all of a sudden — not even your first family. When your mom and dad got married, they had to make a great many adjustments to each other, and when you were born it took them a while to learn how to be parents. You felt very shy with your grandfather until you were about four years old. Now there is a whole new group of people to get to know and to adjust to, and that will take time, too. The one thing you can be sure about is that things will keep changing all the time; *you* will keep changing all the time because you are growing up. Feelings change and people change. When we feel upset or confused or sad and angry, we need to remember that nothing ever stays the same.

There are some special things we learn when a parent dies.* We learn that we need love in order to live, that no one can have a full and happy life unless there is love. We learn that we can withstand more pain than we ever thought was possible, and that there is no useful way to avoid feeling our pain. We learn that nobody ever dies totally, but that

---

* You may want to read another book: *Learning to Say Good-by: When a Parent Dies,* by Eda LeShan (Macmillan, 1976).

everything he or she did while alive remains part of us. But most of all we learn how precious life is, how important it is not to waste it. Sharon notices that since her mother died, she looks at more sunsets and marvels at the beauty; Lenny discovers that he is more curious than ever to study chemistry; Oliver notices that he loves his great-grandfather more than he ever did before because he realizes he probably won't live too many more years. Eli hugs his mother more often; Joan takes a longer time to smell the flowers in her mother's garden. Every day seems more important than ever before. The death of a parent makes you realize just how important you are, for you are the future, you are the next generation. You are the one who will always remember.

7

Going On with Your Life

Mary's mother hasn't had a recurrence of cancer for three years; Mary almost never thinks about the time she was so scared. Pedro's father sits in a wheelchair and doesn't go to work anymore because of his back operation, but the doctor says he should have a long life. Chin Lee's father has died. Ivan's mother is in a mental hospital and nobody knows if she will ever come home or not. Sidney's mother gets better some of the time and then gets worse; she has multiple sclerosis and no one can tell exactly what will happen.

There is one very important thing that all these children have in common: no matter what has happened or will happen to their parents, they are growing and changing every day. Soon they will all be teenagers and will probably feel pretty uncomfortable and shy about the changes that take place in their bodies. Chances are they will feel that they are being treated like babies when they can perfectly well take care of themselves. They will begin to think about what kind of work they would like to do when they grow up. They will even fall in love! At first it may be pretty frightening to think about what it will be like to be a young adult, but after a while, it begins to feel good. During adolescence most young people are quite surprised to find out how their moods change — almost from one minute to the next. Usually that has a lot to do with the hormones that lead to changing from a child to a young adult.

When you become a teenager you will probably worry even more than you do now about being just like your friends. What has been happening to you all your life and will continue for the rest of your life is that you are becoming a special person, not exactly like anyone else, and you can go on growing and learning and changing for as long as you live. What you and your friends have in common is that you all have the same opportunities that any child has, to become *yourself*. What that means is that when you are very young you usually judge who you are by what your parents and teachers think about you. Even though you began to say *"No!"* loudly and clearly by the time you were two years old, and even though you have had many arguments with your parents about things you wanted to do, chances are that you try very hard to please the grown-ups you love.

Kenneth's father went to Harvard. When Kenneth was born, he bought a tiny T-shirt with *Harvard* on the front of it. When he got very sick he kept telling Kenneth how wonderful it would be *when* Kenneth went to Harvard. He never said *if,* and after his father died when Kenneth was twelve, Kenneth felt that he would have to follow his father's wishes. The only trouble with that was that Kenneth was very restless and itchy sitting in classrooms. His happiest times were when he visited the garage that his mother's brother owned and Uncle Mitch began teaching him all about motors and different kinds of cars and trucks. Kenneth daydreams about going to a technical high school and becoming a mechanic. He gets a headache whenever he thinks about his father's dream for him.

Hilda's mother talked a lot about not believing in "Women's Lib." Her mother loved staying home and taking care of her family. She loved sewing and cooking and nursing her babies and shopping and putting up new drapes and wallpapering the kitchen. "If you really want to have a happy life," Hilda's mother told her, "find a wonderful man like Daddy and stay home and have lots of children. Don't pay any attention to all these people who say women

have to go out to work or else they are nobodies."
Hilda felt guilty when she was in the seventh grade
and a teacher told her she was very talented in
science and could be an engineer. It sounded like
such a wonderful idea, but she felt as if she had to
be the kind of person her mother had wanted her
to be.

It is true that many parents have special dreams
for their children and sometimes they make their
children feel they must follow those dreams. But it
is equally true that children ought not to pay too
much attention to their parents' dreams! When parents really begin to think about it, most of them
realize that they want their children to have their
own dreams. It is hard not to try to influence one's
children, but most people now understand that trying
to satisfy other people rather than oneself always
leads to trouble. The more you try to think about
what will make you feel really good, what will make
you happy, the nicer you will be to other people.
The more you try to think about being the person
you want to be, the less likely it is that you will get
sick, or be mean, or feel depressed. The most unhappy people are the ones who spend all their lives
trying to please other people, never themselves.

There is nothing selfish about wanting to find out
how to be your special self. When a person does
what he or she needs to do, it is more than likely
that he or she will want to help other people be

themselves, too. We need to learn to respect other people, and the best way to do that is to start out by respecting ourselves.

If Kenneth struggles very hard it is possible he might get into Harvard, but if he's doing something he hates, he may become nervous and sick, and chances are he won't be very happy or very good at what he's doing. If Hilda decides that she wants to go to college and study engineering, chances are that she will be a happy person who may very well also want to get married and have children. If she gives up *her* dream and tries to fulfill her mother's dream, she may feel very depressed, and she may get very angry at her husband and children and feel as if she is in a prison.

What you need to remember now, as you are growing up, is that when you are older the time will come when you will be able to follow your own dreams, and that it is a wonderful idea to think and dream about what you want to be when you grow up. Sometimes children who have never lived through a parent's illness find it easier to argue with their parents and let them know what they want to do. If a parent is sick or has died, a child feels guilty about not doing what parents want. You need to remember that the best way you can show love and respect for your parents is to become the grown-up you need to be.

Having a parent who is seriously ill might very

well help you in the struggle to be your best self. You have had more experience than most children in learning to examine how you are feeling. When Jean's father got sick, Jean found out that she felt comforted when she went to the public library and stayed there for hours, reading. She found out that she is a quiet person who doesn't like to be around people all the time. She thinks she might like to be a writer. When Mario's father died, what comforted him the most was being with his special group of friends. He found out that having a club with other boys was the one thing that made him feel really good. He thinks about becoming a policeman or a fireman because he has heard that working with a group like that might be most like a club. When Todd's mother was resting in bed, they both began drawing and Todd was surprised to find out he could make funny cartoons that made his brother laugh. It seemed to be the most fun of anything he had ever done and now he thinks about going to an art school after high school.

Because you had to learn about all the kinds of feelings you were having when painful things were happening, you may now be more experienced in understanding your feelings. That important ability will help you in everything you do; it will help you decide what you want to do when you grow up and make it easier to understand other people as well. Your parent's illness could not stop you from growing. It was not an ending. While nothing will ever be exactly as it was before the illness, all life experiences have an influence on us. Many other things will happen that will change your feelings and ideas. Because you had the courage to live through a parent's illness, you will surely have the courage to go on with your life.

Places to Get
Special Information

American Cancer Society
90 Park Avenue South
New York, NY 10016

Cancer Hot Line
1 800 638-6694

Cancer Care, Inc.
19 West Fifty-sixth Street
New York, NY 10019

American Heart Association
7320 Greenville Avenue
Dallas, TX 75231

National Multiple Sclerosis Society
205 East Forty-second Street
New York, NY 10017

National Hospice Organization
Suite 402
1901 North Fortmyer Drive
Arlington, VA 22209

United States Public Health Service
9000 Rockville Pike
Bethesda, MD 20205

National Mental Health Association
1021 Prince Street
Alexandria, VA 22314

Local Chapter, Reach for Recovery